STUDY GUIDES

Mathematics

Year 6

Mark Patmore
and
Bob Hartman

RISING STARS

Rising Stars UK Ltd, 22 Grafton Street, London W1S 4EX

www.risingstars-uk.com

Every effort has been made to trace copyright holders and obtain their permission for the use of copyright materials. The authors and publisher will gladly receive information enabling them to rectify any error or omission in subsequent editions.

All facts are correct at time of going to press.

Published 2007
Reprinted 2008, 2010
Text, design and layout © Rising Stars UK Ltd.

Design: HL Studios
Illustrations: Oxford Designers and Illustrators
Editorial project management: Dodi Beardshaw
Editorial: Allison Toogood and Joanne Osborn
Cover design: Burville-Riley Design

British Library Cataloguing in Publication Data.
A CIP record for this book is available from the British Library.

ISBN: 978-1-84680-101-3

Printed by Craft Print International Ltd, Singapore

Contents

How to get the best out of this book

Most chapters spread across two pages but some spread over four pages. All chapters focus on one topic and should help you to keep 'On track' and to 'Aim higher'.

Title and **What will you learn?** tell you what you are aiming to learn.

Key facts: set out what you need to know and the ideas you need to understand fully.

Language: help build up your mathematical vocabulary. Remember that some words mean one thing in everyday life and something more special in mathematics.

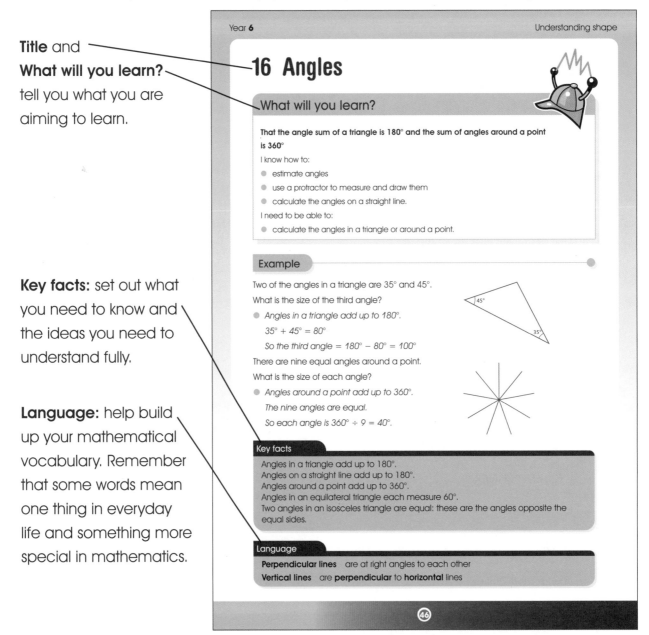

Year **6**   Understanding shape

16 Angles

What will you learn?

That the angle sum of a triangle is 180° and the sum of angles around a point is 360°

I know how to:
- estimate angles
- use a protractor to measure and draw them
- calculate the angles on a straight line.

I need to be able to:
- calculate the angles in a triangle or around a point.

Example

Two of the angles in a triangle are 35° and 45°.
What is the size of the third angle?
- Angles in a triangle add up to 180°.
  35° + 45° = 80°
  So the third angle = 180° − 80° = 100°
There are nine equal angles around a point.
What is the size of each angle?
- Angles around a point add up to 360°.
  The nine angles are equal.
  So each angle is 360° ÷ 9 = 40°.

Key facts

Angles in a triangle add up to 180°.
Angles on a straight line add up to 180°.
Angles around a point add up to 360°.
Angles in an equilateral triangle each measure 60°.
Two angles in an isosceles triangle are equal: these are the angles opposite the equal sides.

Language

Perpendicular lines   are at right angles to each other
Vertical lines   are **perpendicular** to **horizontal** lines

46

Follow these simple rules if you are using the book for revising.

1   Read each page carefully. Give yourself time to take in each idea.

2   Learn the key facts and ideas. If you need help ask your teacher or mum, dad or the adult who looks after you.

3   Concentrate on the things you find more difficult.

4   Only work for about 20 minutes or so at a time. Take a break and then do more work.

If you get most of the **On track** questions right then you know you are working at level 3 or 4. Well done – that's brilliant! If you get most of the **Aiming higher** questions right, you are working at the higher level 4 or 5. You're doing really well!

The **Using and applying** questions are often more challenging and ask you to explain your answers or think of different ways of answering. These questions will be around level 4 or above.

Some questions must be answered without using a calculator – look for 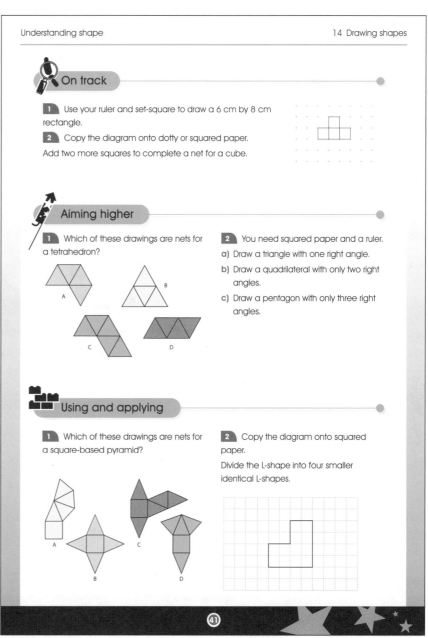. If you are not using a calculator be sure to write down the calculations you are doing. If you are using a calculator remember to try to check your answer to see if it is sensible.

Understanding shape · 14 Drawing shapes

On track

1 Use your ruler and set-square to draw a 6 cm by 8 cm rectangle.

2 Copy the diagram onto dotty or squared paper. Add two more squares to complete a net for a cube.

Aiming higher

1 Which of these drawings are nets for a tetrahedron?

2 You need squared paper and a ruler.
a) Draw a triangle with one right angle.
b) Draw a quadrilateral with only two right angles.
c) Draw a pentagon with only three right angles.

Using and applying

1 Which of these drawings are nets for a square-based pyramid?

2 Copy the diagram onto squared paper.
Divide the L-shape into four smaller identical L-shapes.

41

Follow these simple rules if you want to know how well you are doing.

1 Work through the questions.

2 Keep a record of how well you do.

3 If you are working at level 3 or 4 you will get most of the **On track** questions correct.

4 If you are working at level 4 or 5 you will also get most of the **Aiming higher** questions correct.

1 Negative numbers

What will you learn?

How to find differences between positive and negative numbers

I know how to:

- find the difference between a pair of counting numbers (positive integers)
- position negative numbers on a number line.

I need to be able to:

- find the difference between a positive and a negative integer, or two negative integers.

Example

Here are some city temperatures for the same time on one day in December.

London
4°C

New York
−5°C

Rome
8°C

Moscow
−8°C

Which was the coldest city? Which was the warmest city? How can you tell?

What was the difference in temperature between them?

- *The coldest city was Moscow; the warmest city was Rome.*
- *You could draw a number (temperature) line and mark on each temperature. The difference between them is 16 °C.*

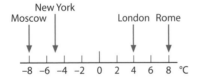

Key facts

Negative numbers are shown to the left of zero on a horizontal number line or below zero on a vertical number line.
If you count along a number line from left to right the numbers get bigger; if you count back from right to left the numbers get smaller.

Language

Positive numbers   numbers greater than zero
Negative numbers   numbers less than zero
Integers   whole numbers

On track

1 Write down the lower temperature in each pair.

a) 0°C, –5°C   b) –1°C, –4°C   c) –36°C, –40°C

2 What temperature is:

a) 3°C below 0°C?   b) 10°C below –10°C?   c) 1°C below 1°C?

3 Temperatures are taken on one day in each of five cities.

City	Temperature at midnight	Temperature at midday
Birmingham	2°C	9°C
Leeds	–2°C	8°C
Newcastle	–7°C	2°C
Norwich	3°C	8°C
Nottingham	–4°C	7°C

a) Which city had the lowest temperature at midnight?

b) Which city had the greatest temperature rise between midnight and midday?

c) Which city had the smallest temperature rise between midnight and midday?

Aiming higher

1 You may need a calculator for this question.

In a magic square the numbers in each column, each row and each diagonal all add up to the same number, called the magic number.

In this magic square there are both positive and negative numbers and the magic number is –6.

–3	+2	–5
–4	–2	0
+1	–6	–1

There are some numbers missing in this magic square.

The magic number is –6 again.

Each column, row and diagonal adds up to –6.

Copy and complete it.

0		
–7	–2	
		–4

Using and applying

1 A sequence **starts at 30**

30
22
14
......

The rule is **keep subtracting 8**

Write the first two numbers in the sequence that are **less than zero**.

How did you find them?

2 Decimals

What will you learn?

How to understand and use decimals with up to three places

I know how to:

- partition, round and order decimals with up to two places
- round large numbers to the nearest multiple of 10, 100 or 1000.

I need to be able to:

- partition decimals with up to three places and position them on a number line
- round decimals to the nearest whole number or nearest tenth.

Example

Round these decimal numbers to the nearest tenth: 2.75   2.052

You can:

*use place value headings: Units (U), ten**ths** (t), hundred**ths** (h), thousand**ths** (th)*

U .	t	h	th
2 .	7	5	
2 .	0	5	2

position the decimal numbers on a number line.

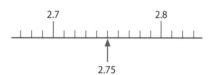

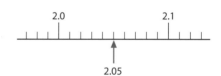

- *2.75 is exactly halfway between 2.7 and 2.8 and the rule is to round up to 2.8.*
- *2.052 is just past 2.05 and is closer to 2.1 than to 2.0, so round up to 2.1.*

Key facts

The value of each digit is given by its position or place.
The decimal point marks the division between whole numbers and the fraction part of a number, e.g. 4.786 is 4 units + 7 tenths + 8 hundredths + 6 thousandths.

Language

Tenths (t)   are $\frac{1}{10}$ of a unit

Hundredths (h)   are $\frac{1}{100}$ of a unit

Thousandths (th)   are $\frac{1}{1000}$ of a unit

To two decimal places   means 'to the nearest hundredth'
Remember: the decimal fraction number names below zero are the same as the names above zero but with 'th' added.

On track

1

10   11

B   A

Write down the values shown by A and B.

3 Round each number to one decimal place.

6.144   23.1577

2 Write these decimals in order, smallest first.

7.7   7.77   7.17   7.707

4 Round each number to the nearest 100.

98   112   275   2052

 **Aiming higher**

1 Round

a) 24.95 to the nearest 10.

b) 314.69 to the nearest whole number.

c) 1678 to the nearest 1000.

d) 4.323 to two decimal places.

2 Which number is closest in value to 0.5?

0.05   0.08   0.11   0.2   0.9

3 Copy and continue each number sequence for the next four numbers:

a) 8.2, 8.4, 8.6, …

b) 9.96, 9.97, 9.98, …

c) 6.03, 6.02, 6.01, …

 Using and applying

1 Katy started with a number and rounded it to the nearest integer.

a) What number might she have started with?

b) What are the smallest and the largest numbers she could have started with?
How do you know?

The answer is 64.

2 Katy lives 6 km, rounded to the nearest kilometre, from school.
What is the longest/shortest distance she might have to walk?

3 Write down a number that lies between 5.13 and 5.19. Which of the two numbers is it closer to? How do you know?

3 Fractions

What will you learn?

How to write one number as a fraction of another, simplify fractions and order them

I know how to:

● find equivalent fractions.

I need to be able to:

● simplify fractions by cancelling common factors

● order fractions by converting them to fractions with a common denominator

● write one number as a fraction of another.

Example

Write these fractions in order, smallest first. $\dfrac{3}{4}$ $\dfrac{4}{5}$ $\dfrac{7}{10}$ $\dfrac{13}{20}$

● *You can make and then compare equivalent fractions by finding a common denominator: a number that all the denominators (4, 5, 10 and 20) divide into exactly. The smallest common denominator is 20.*

Fractions	$\dfrac{3}{4}$	$\dfrac{4}{5}$	$\dfrac{7}{10}$	$\dfrac{13}{20}$
Equivalent fractions	$\dfrac{15}{20}$	$\dfrac{16}{20}$	$\dfrac{14}{20}$	$\dfrac{13}{20}$
So the answer is:	$\dfrac{13}{20}$	$\dfrac{7}{10}$	$\dfrac{3}{4}$	$\dfrac{4}{5}$

● *You can make and then compare equivalent fractions using decimals.*

Using decimals: $\dfrac{7}{10} = 0.7$ $\dfrac{4}{5} = 0.8$ $\dfrac{3}{4} = 0.75$ $\dfrac{13}{20} = 0.65$

So the answer is: $\dfrac{13}{20}$ $\dfrac{7}{10}$ $\dfrac{3}{4}$ $\dfrac{4}{5}$

Which of these fractions is the same as $\frac{4}{5}$?

$$\frac{16}{20}, \quad \frac{12}{18}, \quad \frac{8}{10}, \quad \frac{20}{25}, \quad \frac{24}{30}, \quad \frac{12}{16}$$

● *Either simplify the fractions – finding equivalent fractions:*

$$\frac{16}{20} = \frac{4}{5}, \quad \frac{12}{18} = \frac{2}{3}, \quad \frac{8}{10} = \frac{4}{5}, \quad \frac{20}{25} = \frac{4}{5}, \quad \frac{24}{30} = \frac{4}{5}, \quad \frac{12}{16} = \frac{3}{4}$$

so clearly the only two fractions that need further checking are $\frac{12}{18} = \frac{2}{3}$ *and* $\frac{12}{16} = \frac{3}{4}$

change these to decimals giving $\frac{12}{18} = \frac{2}{3} = 0.6666$ *and* $\frac{12}{16} = \frac{3}{4} = 0.75$. *But* $\frac{4}{5} = 0.8$ *so*

$\frac{12}{18}$ *and* $\frac{12}{16}$ *are not the same as* $\frac{4}{5}$.

How can you tell, just by looking if a fraction is less than or greater than one half?

For example, all of these fractions are less than a half: $\frac{1}{4}, \frac{3}{7}, \frac{4}{9}$

A fraction is less than a half if double the numerator is less than double the denominator.

$$\frac{1}{4} = \frac{2}{8}, \quad \frac{3}{7} = \frac{6}{14}, \quad \frac{4}{9} = \frac{8}{18}$$

Key facts

Equivalent fractions have the same value.
To compare fractions use equivalent fractions with a common denominator or convert them into decimals.
A fraction is in its lowest terms when there is no equivalent fraction with a smaller denominator.

Language

Numerator   the top number of a fraction

Denominator   the bottom number of a fraction

Equivalent   the same value as

Simplify   means write a fraction in its '**lowest terms**' when the numerator and denominator have no more common factors, e.g. $\frac{6}{12}$ is equivalent to $\frac{3}{6}, \frac{2}{4}, \frac{1}{2}$ ...., but simplifying $\frac{6}{12}$, or writing it in its lowest terms, gives the answer $\frac{1}{2}$

Factor   a number that divides exactly into another

Cancel   divide both numbers in a fraction by the same factor

On track

1 Compare these fractions. Write down two that are greater than $\frac{1}{2}$.

$\frac{3}{20}$ $\frac{7}{10}$ $\frac{4}{8}$ $\frac{10}{15}$ $\frac{2}{5}$

2 Copy and complete the equivalent fractions.

$$\frac{3}{5} = \frac{}{15} = \frac{30}{\square}$$

3 Write $\frac{12}{20}$ in its lowest terms.

$$\frac{12}{20} = \frac{\square}{\square}$$

4 Copy the list of fractions.

Some of them are equivalent to $\frac{4}{5}$. Mark these with a ✓ and the rest with a ✗.

$\frac{16}{20}$ $\frac{12}{18}$ $\frac{8}{10}$ $\frac{20}{25}$ $\frac{24}{30}$ $\frac{12}{16}$

Aiming higher

1 Find the fraction that is exactly halfway between $\frac{3}{4}$ and $\frac{5}{6}$.

2 Which fraction is larger? $\frac{2}{3}$ or $\frac{3}{5}$

Show your working.

3 **a)** Choose pairs of numbers to make as many fractions as you can.

    2   5   7   9

b) Put your fractions in order, smallest first.

c) Look at the numerators and denominators. Describe any patterns you can see.

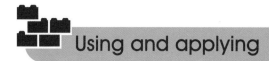

Using and applying

1 Write down two fractions with a difference of $\frac{3}{4}$.

Each fraction must be greater than zero and less than 1.

Explain how you did it.

2 Harry makes a fraction with two number cards.

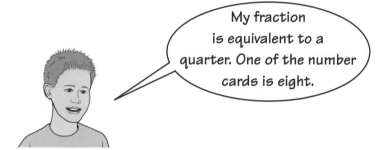

My fraction is equivalent to a quarter. One of the number cards is eight.

What could Harry's fraction be? How many answers can you find?

3 Here are some number cards.

$$3 \quad 5 \quad 7 \quad 9 \quad 11$$

a) Use two of the cards to make a fraction less than $\frac{1}{2}$.

b) How much less than 1 is your fraction?

4 Which of these fractions is the same as $\frac{4}{5}$?

$$\frac{16}{20} \qquad \frac{12}{18} \qquad \frac{8}{10} \qquad \frac{20}{25} \qquad \frac{24}{30} \qquad \frac{12}{16}$$

5 How can you tell, just by looking, if a fraction is less than or greater than one half?

For example, all these fractions are less than a half:

$$\frac{1}{4} \qquad \frac{3}{7} \qquad \frac{4}{9}$$

4 Percentages

What will you learn?

How to work with percentages, decimals and fractions, and work out one quantity as a percentage of another

I know that:

- a percentage is another way of writing a fraction with a denominator of 100, e.g. $50\% = \frac{50}{100} = \frac{1}{2}$

- $\frac{1}{100} = 1\%$ and $\frac{1}{10} = 10\%$.

I need to be able to:

- write one quantity as a percentage of another

- find equivalent percentages, decimals and fractions.

Example

What is £30 as a percentage of £120?

Write £30 out of £120 as a fraction (denominator £120).

Change into a percentage by multiplying by 100.

$$\frac{£30}{£120} \times 100 = 25\%$$

Which fraction is equivalent to 30%? $\frac{1}{3}$ $\frac{1}{30}$ $\frac{3}{10}$ $\frac{1}{300}$

30% means $\frac{30}{100}$. *This fraction is equivalent to* $\frac{3}{10}$.

Key facts

A percentage is a fraction with a denominator of 100.
Change fractions into percentages by multiplying by 100%.
Change percentages into fractions by dividing by 100.
Change fractions into decimals by dividing the numerator by the denominator.

Language

Percentage   per hundred ('century' means 100 years or 100 runs in cricket)
Numerator   the top number of a fraction
Denominator   the bottom number of a fraction
Equivalent   the same value as

On track

1 Which two fractions are equivalent to 0.7?

$\frac{7}{10}$ $\frac{1}{70}$ $\frac{70}{100}$ $\frac{1}{7}$

2 **a)** $\frac{2}{4}$ and $\frac{4}{8}$ are fractions equivalent to 50%. Write another fraction equal to 50%.

b) $\frac{4}{5}$ and $\frac{8}{10}$ are fractions equivalent to 80%. Write another fraction equal to 80%.

3 12 out of 60 MP3 players need new batteries after one year.
What percentage is this?

4 Write these as percentages.

a) 16 out of 50   **b)** 5 kg out of 200 kg

c) 3 cm out of 12 cm   **d)** 4 litres out of 25 litres

e) 800 g out of 4 kg   (Be careful of the units!)

5

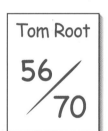

Amy gets 48 marks out of 60 in a test. Tom gets 56 marks out of 70 in a different test.

Who scored the highest percentage? Show your working.

6 **a)** What percentage of £10 is £2?

b) What percentage of £2 is £10?

7 **a)** Write down the numbers in the list with a value **greater than a half**.

10% $\frac{48}{100}$ 6% $\frac{6}{10}$ $\frac{51}{100}$ 60%

b) Write down the numbers in this list with a value **greater than 75%**.

$\frac{3}{4}$ $\frac{7}{10}$ $\frac{8}{100}$ $\frac{70}{100}$ $\frac{8}{10}$ $\frac{55}{100}$

Aiming higher

1 **a)** Write a **percentage** that is **greater than** $\frac{8}{10}$ and **less than** $\frac{90}{100}$.

b) Write a **decimal** that is **greater than** 25% and **less than** 50%.

c) Write a **decimal** that is **greater than** $\frac{1}{2}$ and **less than** 75%.

2 Pair each decimal in row A with a percentage from row B.

A	0.05	0.7	0.5	0.75	4.5	0.075	0.45
B	450%	5%	70%	75%	50%	45%	7.5%

3 What percentages are the following?

a) 2p of £1   **c)** 15 mm of 1 cm   **e)** 100 m of 1 km

b) 1 cm of 1 m   **d)** 50p of £5   **f)** 20 g of 1 kg

4 Children in Year 6 could choose to go to Alton Towers or the seaside for an end-of-term trip. The table shows what happened.

	Alton Towers	Seaside
Girls	24	36
Boys	36	29

a) What was the total number of pupils who chose Alton Towers?

b) What percentage of these were girls?

c) What was the total number of girls in Year 6?

d) What percentage of the girls chose the seaside?

e) What was the total percentage of pupils who chose Alton Towers?

Show your working.

5 Emma makes a fraction with two number cards.

> My fraction
> is equivalent to 25%.
> One of my cards is 8.

What could the other card be?

Using and applying

1 **a)** Sort these numbers into two sets.

60%   0.6 $\frac{7}{5}$ $\frac{3}{5}$ 140%   1.40

b) Explain how you grouped the numbers.

c) Write one more fraction in each set.

2 **a)** Twenty out of a hundred men are colour blind.

What percentage are not colour blind?

b) World-wide, 37 out of 100 people are under 20 years old.

What percentage of people in the world are 20 years or more old?

c) In 2005, four out of every ten people in Africa lived in a city.

What percentage of people in Africa did not live in a city?

d) Nine out of ten children play games on the Internet.

What percentage of children do not play games on the Internet?

3 Look at this pattern made from squares.

a) What percentage of the squares is shaded?

b) Can you shade in more squares so that 80% of the squares are shaded and the pattern still has reflective symmetry?

5 Proportion and ratio

What will you learn?

How to solve ratio and proportion problems by scaling quantities up or down

I know how to:

- use doubling and halving, and other simple sequences, to scale numbers up or down
- change the quantities in a recipe for fewer or more people.

I need to be able to:

- scale any quantity up or down to solve a simple problem.

Example

Three pens cost 84 pence. How much do five pens cost?

Here are two possible ways of solving this problem.

Find what one pen costs: *1 pen costs 84p ÷ 3 = 28p.*

Then find what five pens cost: *5 pens cost 28p × 5 = £1.40*

Write down this fraction: $\dfrac{\text{new number}}{\text{old number}}$

Multiply the cost by the fraction: $84p \times \dfrac{5}{3} = £1.40$

*The new number is larger than the old number, so you are **scaling up**.*

Key facts

The simplest way to solve ratio and proportion problems is to find the value, or cost, of one thing and then multiply by the new number of things.

Doubling and halving are also useful techniques.

E.g. If 200 g of sherbert lemons cost £1.80, how much do 150 g cost?

Halve to find cost of 100 g: 90p
Halve again to find cost of 50 g: 45p
Add to find cost of 150 g: £1.35

Language

Ratio   compares a part to a part

Proportion   compares a part to the whole

E.g. in a class of 30 children, there are 20 boys and 10 girls.

The **ratio** of boys to girls is 20 to 10 or 2 to 1, which is often written as 2:1

The **proportion** of boys in the class is 20 out of 30 or 2 out of 3, which is usually written as $\dfrac{2}{3}$.

On track

1 Amy is making strawberry ice cream for ten people.

a) What weight of strawberries will she need?

b) How much sugar will she need?

> **Strawberry ice cream for six people**
> 600 g strawberries   200 ml cream
> 240 g sugar   100 ml water

2 In a zoo there are 30 monkeys and some gorillas and chimpanzees.

The ratio of monkeys to gorillas is 6 to 1.

The ratio of monkeys to chimpanzees is 5 to 2.

a) How many gorillas are there?   b) How many chimpanzees are there?

Twelve monkeys are moved to another zoo.

What are the new ratios of:

c) monkeys to gorillas?   d) monkeys to chimpanzees?

Aiming higher

1 Amy is making a necklace from black and white beads.

She makes groups of three black beads and two white beads.

Each group is followed by a silver disc. The picture shows part of the necklace.

2 Amy has 45 black beads to use. Work out how many of the others she needs.

a) white beads   b) silver discs

Using and applying

1 Here is a way to make purple paint.

Mix red paint and blue in the ratio 4 to 1.

a) How much red paint do you mix with 50 ml of blue paint?

b) How much blue paint do you mix with 1200 ml of red paint?

Show how you worked your answers out.

2 Zaphyr bought 50 m of climbing rope for £80.

a) How much would 150 m of climbing rope cost?

b) How much rope could he get for £100?

Show how you worked your answers out.

6 Using place value

What will you learn?

How to use tables facts to work out other facts

I know:

● tables facts to 10 × 10.

I need to be able to:

● use tables facts with decimals to work out, e.g. 0.4 × 8 and 5.6 ÷ 7.

Example

214 × 74 = 158.36

Some decimal points have been left out of this question but the answer is correct.

Use the fact that 214 × 74 = 15,836 to put in decimal points to make the calculation correct.

15,836 ÷ 100 = 158.36

So, to make the calculation correct, we need to:

> *divide 214 by 100;*

or *divide 74 by 100;*

or *divide both 214 and 74 by 10.*

This gives: 2.14 × 74 = 158.36

or 214 × 0.74 = 158.36

or 21.4 × 7.4 = 158.36

Key facts

Multiplying by 10 moves digits one column to the left;
multiplying by 100 moves digits two columns to the left...
Dividing by 10 moves digits one column to the right;
dividing by 100 moves digits two columns to the right...

Language

Tenths (t) are $\frac{1}{10}$ of a unit

Hundredths (h) are $\frac{1}{100}$ of a unit

Thousandths (th) are $\frac{1}{1000}$ of a unit

Remember: the decimal fraction number names below zero are the same as the names above zero but with 'th' added.

On track

 1 The answer to a calculation is 0.64.

Write down two possible calculations that will give the answer 0.64.

 2 **a)** What number divided by 6 gives 4.2? **b)** What is 0.56 ÷ 7?

3 Amy knows that 156 × 36 = 5616.

The answers to the following sums are wrong.

Where could she put decimal points to make the answers correct?

a) 156 × 36 = 56.16

b) 156 × 36 = 561.6

c) 156 × 36 = 5.616

d) 156 × 36 = 0.5616

Aiming higher

1 Use your calculator, but don't use ÷.

Find the missing numbers.

a) ☐ × 16 = 24 **b)** ☐ × 15 = 33

2 Amy works out 123 × 456 = 56,088.

12.3 x 45.6 must be 56.088.

That's not right!

 How does Amy know this, just by looking at the answer?

What is the correct answer?

Using and applying

 1 **a)** Write down the factors of 30.

There are eight in total including 1 and 30.

b) Ignore 1 and 30 and choose two other factors, e.g. 5 and 15.

You can multiply and divide these numbers like this:

$$5 \times 15 = 75 \qquad 5 \div 15 = \frac{1}{3}$$

$$15 \div 5 = 3$$

Show how you can use these facts to make these answers.

7.5 0.75 0.3 30

7 Using multiplication facts

What will you learn?

How to work out squares of numbers

I know:

- tables facts to 10×10.

I need to be able to find:

- squares of numbers to 12×12
- squares of multiples of 10.

Example

Estimate the answer to 31×29.

31 is very close to 30 and 29 is very close to 30, so a good estimate is
$30 \times 30 = 900$.

The square of a two-digit number is close to 2000. What two-digit number could it be?

$40 \times 40 = 40 \times 4 \times 10 = 1600$, and $50 \times 50 = 2500$, so the number will be
between 40 and 50.

You could find it by trying different numbers but an efficient way is to think about the
grid method of multiplication:

	40	1	
40	1600	40	1640
1	40	1	41
			1681

This grid shows $41 \times 41 = 1681$.

If you changed the numbers to 42×42, you would
keep 1600 and add $80 + 80 + 4 = 1764$.

If you changed the numbers to 43×43, you would
keep 1600 and add $120 + 120 + 9 = 1849$.

Keeping going, $44^2 = 1936$ and $45^2 = 2025$ and so
the number could be 44 or 45.

Key fact

You can make a square number by multiplying any number by itself.
E.g. $15^2 = 15 \times 15 = 225$ and 225 is a square number.

Language

Square number is a number that can be drawn as a square array of dots

Squaring means multiplying a number by itself

On track

1 Write down two square numbers that total:

a) 25   b) 169

2 Find two square numbers that multiply together to give 144.

Can you find another pair?

3 Use the fact that $7 \times 7 = 49$ to write down the value of 70^2.

Aiming higher

1 Estimate the area of a rectangular field that is 52 m long and 49 m wide.

2 Look at this pattern.

$$1 + 3 = 2^2$$
$$1 + 3 + 5 = 3^2$$
$$1 + 3 + 5 + 7 = 4^2$$

a) What do you notice?

b) Use the pattern to copy and complete this number sentence.

$$1 + 3 + 5 + 7 + 9 + 11 + 13 = \boxed{}^2 = \boxed{}$$

c) Write down a similar sum that equals 11^2.

3 Odd square numbers can be made by adding two consecutive numbers.

E.g. $3^2 = 4 + 5$ $5^2 = 12 + 13$ $7^2 = 24 + 25$

a) What number squared $= 60 + 61$?

b) What two consecutive numbers add to give 13^2?

Using and applying

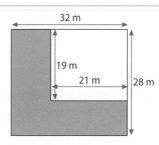

32 m

19 m

21 m

28 m

1 Look at the diagram.

Estimate the area of the shaded L-shape.

Show your working.

2 Arash rolls two dice.

One dice is numbered 1 to 6 and the other is numbered 3 to 8.

The two rolled numbers are used to make a two-digit number.

E.g. 35 or 53

Which square numbers could Arash make?

8 Prime numbers

What will you learn?

To identify prime numbers up to 100, and to find prime factors

I know how to:

● find pairs of factors of two-digit whole numbers.

I need to be able to:

● use this to find out whether a number is a prime number

● identify the prime factors.

Example

Write a number with prime factors 5 and 7.

The answer could be $5 \times 7 = 35$

$5 \times 5 \times 7 = 175$

$5 \times 7 \times 7 = 245$

$5 \times 7 \times 5 \times 7 = 1225$

or any number made by multiplying 5s and 7s.

Find the prime factors of 36.

You can use a factor tree to find the prime factors of a number.

Here is the factor tree for 36.

Begin with 36 at the top.

Underneath write a factor pair for 36,

e.g. 12 and 3.

If either factor is not prime, continue by writing another factor pair underneath,

e.g. 3 and 4 below 12. (Notice that 3 is prime, so just repeat it.)

Keep drawing the tree like this until there are only prime numbers in the bottom row.

So $36 = 3 \times 2 \times 2 \times 3$, and the prime factors of 36 are 2 and 3.

Key facts

A prime number has exactly two factors which means it can only be divided exactly by itself and 1. The number 1 is not a prime number because it has only one factor.

Language

Factors   are numbers that divide **exactly** into other numbers (no remainder)
E.g. 3 is a factor of 6 because 3 divides exactly into 6.
Prime factors   are the factors that are prime numbers

On track

1 **a)** Write down the factors of 12, 14 and 20, and then 4, 9 and 16.

b) What do you notice about the number of factors each of the square numbers has?

c) Investigate some more square numbers.

2 **a)** Copy and complete this factor tree for 56.

b) Now write down the prime factors of 56.

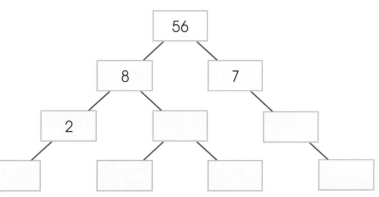

 Aiming higher

1 **a)** The number 1 is not a prime number. Can you explain why?

b) Are there any even prime numbers apart from 2? Can you explain why?

2 13 is a prime number and so is 31. List all the other two-digit prime numbers that are still prime when their digits are reversed.

 Using and applying

1 Find three prime numbers to multiply together to give a product of:

a) 105   **b)** 385.

Show how you worked out your answers.

2

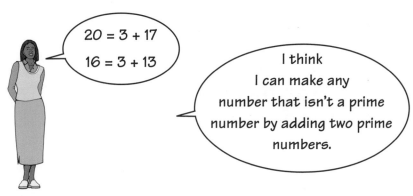

$20 = 3 + 17$

$16 = 3 + 13$

I think I can make any number that isn't a prime number by adding two prime numbers.

Try some other numbers and see if you think this is always possible.

9 Checking results

What will you learn?

How to estimate and check the calculations that I do in several ways

I know how:

- to round numbers
- to use different methods of calculation
- different numbers behave when I use them in calculations.

I need to be able to:

- use estimates so that I know what sort of answer to expect
- choose an appropriate way of checking my answer.

Example

Check the answer to 532×7.

Here are two possible methods of working out the answer. You can use one way to check the other.

- $532 \times 7 = (532 \times 10) - (532 \times 3)$
- $532 \times 7 = (500 \times 7) + (32 \times 7)$

Fill in the boxes to check the answer to 496×8 in the same way.

$496 \times 8 = (\boxed{} \times 10) - (496 \times \boxed{})$

$496 \times 8 = (500 \times \boxed{}) - (\boxed{} \times \boxed{})$

- $496 \times 8 = (\mathbf{496} \times 10) - (496 \times \mathbf{2})$
- $496 \times 8 = (500 \times \mathbf{8}) - (\mathbf{4} \times \mathbf{8})$

Key facts

Round up or down to estimate. Remember to round up if the last digit is 5 or more.

Common-sense rules, e.g.

if you multiply by an even number the answer is even

all numbers with the last digit 5 or 0 can be divided by 5

if a number is divisible by 9, it is also divisible by 3 because $9 = 3 \times 3$.

Some tests for dividing numbers exactly:

by 3: add up the digits and the total will be divisible by 3, e.g. 27 is divisible by 3 because $2 + 7 = 9$ and $9 \div 3 = 3$; 35 is not divisible by 3 because $3 + 5 = 8$.

by 4: divide the last two digits by 4 and there will be no remainder, e.g. 1932 is divisible by 4 because 4 divides exactly into 32.

Language

Factors are numbers that divide **exactly** into other numbers (no remainder)
E.g. 4 is a factor of 16 because 4 divides exactly into 16.
Another way of expressing this is that 16 is **divisible by** 4.

On track

1. What is a good approximation for 5.7×19.4? Explain why.

2. Is 5 a factor of 840? How do you know?

3. Hannah adds five odd numbers together and gets an even answer.

How do you know she has made a mistake?

4. Here are some calculations. All the answers are incorrect.

Write down how you can tell this.

a) $123 \times 45 = 5534$ ✗   b) $456 \times 97 = 54{,}232$ ✗

c) $816 \times 52 = 32{,}432$ ✗   d) $315 \times 41 = 12{,}910$ ✗

Aiming higher

1. The answer to $358 \div 4$ lies between $360 \div 4 = 90$ and $320 \div 4 = 80$.

Show how you know the answer to $547 \div 8$ lies between 60 and 70.

2. a) Which of these numbers is divisible by 3?

   83   102   257   1137   4196   200,736

b) Which of these numbers is divisible by 4?

   124   421   4082   4096   11,334

3. Find the smallest number that must be added to 222,223 to make it divisible by

a) 3   b) 4

4. How do you know that 234 is divisible by 9?

Using and applying

1. a) $3400 + 1265 = 4665$

    Rukhsana checks the answer to this sum by
    calculating $4000 + 665$.

    How did she get these numbers?

b) Use the same method to check $2700 + 948 = 3648$.

2. **294** has 2 and 7 as factors.

Write another three-digit number with 2 and 7 as factors.

10 Calculating efficiently

What will you learn?

How to use efficient written methods to add, subtract, multiply and divide integers and decimal numbers

I know how to use efficient written methods to:

● add and subtract whole numbers and decimals with up to two places

● multiply and divide whole numbers and decimals with one place by a one-digit number.

I need to be able to use efficient written methods to:

● calculate the answer to HTU ÷ U and U.t ÷ U to one or two decimal places.

Example

You can use any of the standard methods to multiply or divide.

Debbie buys a pack of 24 cartons of drink for £4.80.

What is the cost of each carton?

● *Each carton costs £4.80 ÷ 24 = 480 ÷ 24 = 20 pence.*

Carl has £4.50 to spend on chocolate.

How many bars of chocolate can he buy if each bar costs 75p?

● *Number of bars = 450 ÷ 75 = 6.*

You may find this easier to work backwards.

You know that 2 × 75 = 150 and that 3 × 150 = 450, so he can buy 2 × 3 = 6 bars.

Tom buys seven DVDs for £87.50. How much does each one cost?

```
7)87.5
−70.0        10 × 7
  17.5
  14.0         2 × 7
   3.5
   3.5       0.5 × 7
   0.0
  answer £12.50
```

Key fact

Remember to line up the decimal points when you add or subtract decimal numbers.

Language

Integers   are whole numbers

On track

 1 Find the answers to these calculations:

a) $3.72 \div 3$ b) $3.65 \div 5$ c) $1.84 \div 8$ d) $18.4 \div 8$

 2 A bottle of orange juice holds 0.75 litres. Mrs Jones wants 9 litres of juice for a party. How many bottles does she need?

 3 Michael has three number cards and a card with a decimal point.

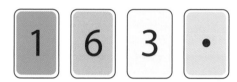

a) What is the largest number Michael can make with all four cards?

b) What is the smallest number he can make with all four cards?

c) Sonny puts **3.61** into his calculator.

He **multiplies** this number by **10**.

What number should he see on the calculator display?

d) Kate puts **31.6** into her calculator.

She **divides** this number by **100**.

What number should she see on the calculator display?

Aiming higher

1 Look at this number chain.

Copy and complete these chains.

a)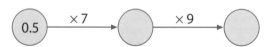

b)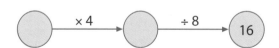

Using and applying

 1 Two numbers have a difference of 2.678.

One of the numbers is 4.369.

What could the other number be? Is there more than one possible answer?

 2 In these divisions each letter represents a missing digit.

Find the missing digits. Explain how you did it.

a)
$$\begin{array}{r} 26 \\ 3\overline{)A8} \end{array}$$

b)
$$\begin{array}{r} LM5 \\ 3\overline{)97N} \end{array}$$

11 Finding fractions and percentages

What will you learn?

How to find fractions and percentages of whole numbers

I know how to:

- use division to find fractions of whole numbers
- find simple percentages.

I need to be able to:

- relate fractions to multiplication and division
- find fractions and percentages of whole-number quantities.

Example

30% of cheddar cheese is fat.

Calculate the amount of fat in 250 g of cheddar cheese.

- 30% is 3 × 10% and 10% = $\frac{1}{10}$

  $\frac{1}{10}$ of 250 = 25, so 30% = 3 × $\frac{1}{10}$ = 75 g

or

- 30% = $\frac{30}{100}$ = 0.3

  So 30% of 250 g = 0.3 × 250 g = 75 g

Find $\frac{2}{3}$ of £24.

- $\frac{2}{3}$ of £24 = $\frac{2}{3}$ × £24 = 2 × $\frac{1}{3}$ × £24 = 2 × £8 = £16

Key facts

A percentage is a fraction with a denominator of 100.
Change fractions into percentages by multiplying by 100.
Change percentages into fractions by dividing by 100.
Change fractions into decimals by dividing the numerator by the denominator.
E.g. $\frac{3}{4}$ as a percentage is $\frac{3}{4}$ × 100% = 75%. $\frac{3}{4}$ as a decimal is 3 ÷ 4 = 0.75.

Language

Percentage   per hundred ('century' means 100 years or 100 runs in cricket)

Numerator   the top number of a fraction

Denominator   the bottom number of a fraction

Equivalent   the same value as

On track

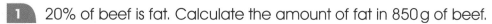

1 20% of beef is fat. Calculate the amount of fat in 850g of beef.

2 Copy and complete these sentences.

a) 20% of 80 is ____.   b) 20% of ____ is 80.

3 Sam asked 40 children in his school for their favourite crisp flavour.

Flavour	Number of children
plain	8
salt and vinegar	10
cheese and onion	4
barbeque	18

What flavour did 20% of the children choose?

4 A bag has 36 coloured balls in it.

Four balls are blue, $\frac{3}{4}$ of the balls are red and the rest are green.

a) How many green balls are there?

b) Three more green balls are added to the bag.

What fraction of the balls are green now?

5 Find:

a) $\frac{3}{4}$ of £48   b) 40% of £750   c) 25% of 44m

6 Write down answers to the following calculations:

a) $\frac{2}{5}$ of £2.50   b) $\frac{3}{4}$ of £4.80   c) $\frac{3}{10}$ of 2 litres

7 Flowers in a garden display are arranged in the following proportions:

red   10%
yellow   35%
pink   20%
purple   25%
white   10%

There are 200 flowers altogether.

Find how many there are of each colour.

8 David and Mary played a game with some fraction cards.

| $\frac{1}{10}$ | $\frac{1}{3}$ | $\frac{1}{20}$ | $\frac{2}{8}$ | $\frac{6}{10}$ | $\frac{1}{100}$ | $\frac{60}{100}$ | $\frac{25}{50}$ | $\frac{3}{5}$ | $\frac{4}{8}$ |

They decided to sort the cards into three groups.

Write which fraction they should place in each group.

Less than half	A half	More than half

Aiming higher

1 **a)** At a wildlife park the butterfly house has a picture of a butterfly on the wall.

On the picture the butterfly is 240 mm wide.

The width of the real butterfly is 20% of 240 mm. How wide is the real butterfly?

b) Inside the butterfly house is a sign with a beetle on it.

On the sign the beetle is 100 mm long. The real beetle is $\frac{1}{4}$ of this length.
How long is the real beetle?

2 Copy and complete these statements.

a) 20 is 10% of _____.   **c)** 4 is 25% of _____.

b) 12 is 60% of _____.   **d)** 120 is 80% of _____.

3 Here is a set of cards.

| 10 | 20 | 25 | 40 | 50 | % | of | = |

Try to put them together to make at least four correct statements.

E.g.

| 40 | % | of | 25 | = | 10 |

4 In class 6 70% of the children eat school dinners. 60% of those who eat school dinners like meat pie. What percentage of the children in class 6 stay for school dinners and like meat pie?

Mathematics Study Guide: Year 6

Answer Booklet

Unit 1 Negative numbers
On track
1 a) –5°C
  b) –4°C
  c) –40°C
2 a) –3°C
  b) –20°C
  c) 0°C
3 a) Newcastle
  b) Nottingham
  c) Norwich

Aiming higher
1

0	–1	–5
–7	–2	+3
+1	–3	–4

Using and applying
1 –2, –10
  e.g. 'by jumping backwards along a number line' or 'by subtracting 8 each time in my head' or 'by going through the eight-times table backwards and taking 2 off each answer'.

Unit 2 Decimals
On track
1 A = 10.7, B = 9.5
2 7.7, 7.707, 7.17, 7.77
3 6.1, 23.2
4 100, 100, 300, 2100

Aiming higher
1 a) 20
  b) 315
  c) 2000
  d) 4.32
2 0.2
3 a) 8.2, 8.4, 8.6, **8.8, 9.0, 9.2, 9.4**
  b) 9.96, 9.97, 9.98, **9.99, 10.00, 10.01, 10.02**
  c) 6.03, 6.02, 6.01, **6.00, 5.99, 5.98, 5.97**

Using and applying
1 a) Any number equal to or greater than 63.5 and less than 64.5
  b) The smallest is 63.5 and the largest is 64.49 because 63.5 will round up to 64 and 64.5 will round up to 65
2 5.5 km or 6.4 km
3 Check answers

Unit 3 Fractions
On track
1 $\frac{7}{10}$ and $\frac{10}{15}$
2 $\frac{3}{5} = \frac{9}{15} = \frac{30}{50}$
3 $\frac{12}{20} = \frac{3}{5}$
4 $\frac{16}{20}$ ✓ $\frac{12}{18}$ ✗ $\frac{8}{10}$ ✓ $\frac{20}{25}$ ✓ $\frac{24}{30}$ ✓ $\frac{12}{16}$ ✗

Aiming higher
1 $\frac{19}{24}$
2 $\frac{2}{3}$

3 a) $\frac{2}{9}, \frac{2}{7}, \frac{2}{5}, \frac{5}{9}, \frac{5}{7}, \frac{7}{9}, \frac{7}{5}, \frac{9}{7}, \frac{5}{2}, \frac{7}{2}, \frac{9}{2}$
  b) The order of the numerators is the reverse order of the denominators.

Using and applying
1 e.g. $\frac{11}{12}$ and $\frac{2}{12}$ ($\frac{1}{6}$).
  e.g. think of a small fraction and add $\frac{3}{4}$ to find the second fraction
2 $\frac{2}{8}$ or $\frac{8}{32}$
3 a) Possible answers are $\frac{3}{11}, \frac{5}{11}, \frac{3}{9}, \frac{3}{7}$.
  b) Differences from 1 are $\frac{8}{11}, \frac{6}{11}, \frac{6}{9}, \frac{4}{7}$.
4 Either simplify the fractions – finding equivalent fractions:
  $\frac{16}{20} = \frac{4}{5}, \frac{12}{18} = \frac{2}{3}, \frac{8}{10} = \frac{4}{5}, \frac{20}{25} = \frac{4}{5}, \frac{24}{30} = \frac{4}{5}, \frac{12}{16} = \frac{3}{4}$
  so clearly the only two fractions that need further checking are $\frac{12}{18} = \frac{2}{3}$ and $\frac{12}{16} = \frac{3}{4}$.
  Change these to decimals giving $\frac{12}{18} = \frac{2}{3} = 0.6666$ and $\frac{12}{16} = \frac{3}{4} = 0.75$. But $\frac{4}{5} = 0.8$ so $\frac{12}{18}$ and $\frac{12}{16}$ are not the same as $\frac{4}{5}$.
5 A fraction is less than a half if double the numerator is less than double the denominator.
  $\frac{1}{4} = \frac{2}{8}, \frac{3}{7} = \frac{6}{14}, \frac{4}{9} = \frac{8}{18}$

Unit 4 Percentages
On track
1 $\frac{7}{10}$ and $\frac{70}{100}$
2 a) e.g. $\frac{3}{6}, \frac{6}{12}$
  b) e.g. $\frac{16}{20}, \frac{80}{100}$
3 20%
4 a) 32%; b) 2.5%; c) 25%; d) 16%; e) 20%
5 They both got the same.
  48 ÷ 60 = 80%, 56 ÷ 70 = 80%
6 a) 20%;
  b) 500%
7 a) $\frac{6}{10}, \frac{51}{100}$, 60%
  b) $\frac{8}{10}$

Aiming higher
1 a) e.g. between 80.1% and 89.9%
  b) e.g. between 0.251 and 0.499
  c) e.g. between 0.51 and 0.7499
2 0.05, 5%; 0.7, 70%; 0.5, 50%; 0.75, 75%; 4.5, 450%; 0.075, 7.5%; 0.45, 45%
3 a) 2%
  b) 1%
  c) 150%
  d) 10%
  e) 10%
  f) 2%
4 a) 60
  b) 40%
  c) 60
  d) 60%
  e) 48%
5 2 or 32

Using and applying
1 Set 1
  a) 60%, 0.6, $\frac{3}{5}$

  b) all equivalent to 60%
  c) Extra fraction is, e.g. $\frac{6}{10}$ or $\frac{12}{20}$
Set 2
  a) $\frac{7}{5}$, 140%, 1.4
  b) all equivalent to $\frac{7}{5}$
  c) Extra fraction is, e.g. $\frac{14}{10}$
2 a) 80%
  b) 63%
  c) 60%
  d) 10%
3 a) 60%
  b) check drawing for symmetry – mirror line through middle column of squares

Unit 5 Proportion and ratio
On track
1 a) 1000 g or 1 kg of strawberries
  b) 400 g sugar
2 30 monkeys means there are
  a) 5 gorillas
  b) 12 chimpanzees
  c) 18 monkeys to 5 gorillas is 18 to 5
  d) 18 monkeys to 12 chimpanzees is 3 to 2

Aiming higher
1 There are 15 groups of beads, so
  a) 30 white
  b) 15 silver

Using and applying
1 a) 200 ml of red paint
  b) 300 ml of blue paint
2 a) e.g. 50 m cost £80. 150 = 3 x 50
    3 x £80 = £240
  b) £80 gets 50 m so £1 gets $\frac{50}{80}$ m ⟶
    £100 gets $\frac{50}{80}$ x 100 = 62.5 m

Unit 6 Using place value
On track
1 e.g. 0.32 x 2; 0.32 + 0.32; 0.16 x 4; 1 – 0.36
2 a) 25.2
  b) 0.08
3 a) 56.16 could be 1.56 x 36, or 15.6 x 3.6, or 156 x 0.36
  b) 561.6 could be 15.6 x 36 or 156 x 3.6
  c) 5.616 could be 1.56 x 3.6 or 15.6 x 0.36
  d) 0.5616 could be 0.156 x 3.6 or 1.56 x 0.36

Aiming higher
1 a) 1.5
  b) 2.2
2 e.g. 12 x 40 = 480 so 12.3 x 45.6 must be greater than 480

Using and applying
1 a) 1, 2, 3, 5, 6, 10, 15, 30
  b) e.g. 5 x 1.5 = 7.5; 0.5 x 1.5 = 0.75; 1.5 ÷ 5 = 0.3; 15 ÷ 0.5 = 30

Unit 7 Using multiplication facts
On track
1 a) 9 and 16
   b) 25 and 144
2 9 x 16; 36 x 4
3 $70^2 = 7$ x 10 x 7 x 10 = 7^2 x 100 = 4900

Aiming higher
1 $50^2 = 2500$ square metres
2 a) the number of terms added together gives the number to be squared,
   so 1 + 3 + 5 + 7 ➝ 4 terms so the answer is 4^2
   b) 1 + 3 + 5 + 7 + 9 + 11 + 13 ➝ 7 terms so add up to $7^2 = 49$
   c) 1 + 3 + 5 + 7 + 9 + 11 + 13 + 15 + 17 + 19 + 21 = $11^2 = 121$
3 a) 60 + 61 = 11^2;
   b) 84 + 85 = 169

Using and applying
1 32 x 28 is approximately 30 x 30 = 900 square metres, 19 x 21 is approximately 20 x 20 = 400 square metres so shaded area = 500 square metres
2 16, 25, 36, 64, 81

Unit 8 Prime numbers
On track
1 a) 12; factors are 1, 2, 3, 4, 6, 12
      14; factors are 1, 2, 7, 14
      20; factors are 1, 2, 4, 5, 10, 20
      4; factors are 1, 2, 4
      9; factors are 1, 3, 9
      16; factors are 1, 2, 4, 8, 16
   b) Square numbers have an odd number of factors, e.g. 25 has factors of 1, 5, 25
   c) 64 has seven factors which are 1, 2, 4, 8, 16, 32, 64
2 a)

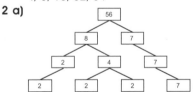

   b) Prime factors of 56 are 2 and 7; 56 = 2 x 2 x 2 x 7. These are some of the non-prime numbers that cannot be made by adding two primes.

Aiming higher
1 a) 1 has only one factor
   b) There are no other even prime numbers because 2 is a factor of all even numbers and so every even number greater than 2 has at least three factors: 1, the number itself and 2.
2 17 ➝ 71; 37 ➝ 73

Using and applying
1 a) 3 x 5 x 7 = 105. 105 has last digit 5 so is a multiple of 5, so possibilities are 7 x 3 x 5 or 3 x 5 x 7.
   b) 385 ends in 5 so is a multiple of 5, so try 5 x 7 x 11.

---

2 No, it is not true. Some numbers where it doesn't work are 27, 35, 51, 65, 77, 87, 93, 95.

Unit 9 Checking results
On track
1 6 x 20; 5.7 is nearly 6 and 19.4 is nearly 20
2 Yes – 840 ends in zero
3 Because odd + odd is even but odd + odd + odd is odd so five odd numbers will be odd
4 a) Must end in 5 because 3 x 5 = 15
   b) Round 456 up to 500 and 97 up to 100 so the answer to 500 x 100 = 50,000 so 456 x 97 will be less than 50,000 so 54,232 must be wrong.
   c) 816 x 52 is more than 800 x 50 which is 40,000
   d) Must end in 5 because 5 x 1 = 5

Aiming higher
1 Lies between 560 ÷ 8 = 70 and 480 ÷ 8 = 60
2 a) 102, 1137, 200,736
   b) 124, 4096
3 a) To be divisible by 3, add 2, giving 222,225;
   b) to be divisible by 4 add 1, giving 222,224
4 Because 2 + 3 + 4 = 9 which is divisible by 3 and therefore by 9

Using and applying
1 a) 3400 + 1265 = 3000 + 400 + 1000 + 265 = 4000 + 665
   b) 2700 + 948 = 2000 + 700 + 900 + 48 = 2000 + 1600 + 48 = 3600 + 48 = 3648
2 2 x 7 = 14 so any number which is a multiple of 14 is acceptable i.e. 140, 280, 294 ...

Unit 10 Calculating efficiently
On track
1 a) 1.24
   b) 0.73
   c) 0.23
   d) 2.3
2 12
3 a) 631
   b) 1.36 or .136
   c) 36.1
   d) 0.316

Aiming higher
1 a) 0.5 x 7 ➝ 3.5 x 9 ➝ 31.5
   b) 32 x 4 ➝ 128 ÷ 8 ➝ 16

Using and applying
1 4.369 + 2.678 = 7.047 or 4.369 – 2.678 = 1.691 so the numbers are 7.047 and 1.691
2 a) A must be 6 or 7 or 8 because 3 into 6, 7 or 8 is 2 with a remainder of 0 or 1 or 2. 6 x 3 = 18 so A must be 7, giving a remainder of 1
   b) L must be 3 (9 ÷ 3 = 3); M must be 2 (7 ÷ 3 = 2 remainder 1); N must be 5 (15 ÷ 3 = 5)

Unit 11 Finding fractions and percentages
On track
1 170 g
2 a) 16
   b) 400
3 plain
4 a) 5 green
   b) $\frac{8}{39}$
5 a) £36
   b) £300
   c) 11 m
6 £1.00, £3.60, 600 ml
7 red = 20, yellow = 70, pink = 40, purple = 50, white = 20
8 less $\frac{1}{10}$, $\frac{1}{3}$, $\frac{1}{20}$, $\frac{2}{8}$, $\frac{1}{100}$
   half $\frac{25}{50}$, $\frac{4}{8}$
   more $\frac{6}{10}$, $\frac{60}{100}$, $\frac{3}{5}$

Aiming higher
1 a) 48 mm
   b) 25 mm
2 a) 200
   b) 20
   c) 16
   d) 150
3 e.g. 50% of 20 = 10; 20% of 50 = 10; 50% of 40 = 20; 25% of 40 = 10
4 42%

Using and applying
1 10% of 720 is 72
   5% of 720 is 36
   2.5% of 720 is 18
   17.5% of 720 is 126
2 Own answers
3 a) £120
   b) £360
   c) £480
   d) £80
4 10% = £8, so 60% = 6 x £8 = £48
   5% = £4, so 65% = £48 + £4 = £52
5 50%

Unit 12 2-D shapes and 3-D solids
On track
1 6 faces, 12 edges, 8 vertices
2 a) 3 cuboids of increasing size;
   b) 8
   c) 16
3

Properties	Triangle
• has one right angle • can be isoscles	right-angled
• all three sides the same length • all three angles the same size (equal to 60°)	equilateral
• two sides equal in length • angles opposite the equal sides are equal	isosceles
• no sides are the same length • no angles are equal	scalene

4 a) two sets of two parallel lines: none
   b) two sets of three parallel lines: A
   c) three sets of two parallel lines: E

1

Quadrilateral	Properties
Square	• Four equal sides • All the angles are right angles
Rectangle	• Two pairs of equal sides • All the angles are right angles
Parallelogram	• Opposite sides are equal and parallel
Rhombus	• Four equal sides • Opposite sides are parallel
Kite	• Two pairs of equal sides; the equal sides are next to each other.
Trapezium	• One pair of parallel sides

2 A right-angled triangle; B equilateral triangle; C parallelogram; D trapezium; E rhombus

3 a) ABGF
b) C and D; H and I

Using and applying
1 Check work, e.g. C moves to (9, 7) and produces a parallelogram. C moves to (10, 4) and produces a triangle.
2 a) 4 faces and 4 vertices; a tetrahedron
b) 6 faces and 6 vertices
c) Number of faces = number of vertices = number of sides of base +1

Unit 13 Co-ordinates and shapes
On track
1 (6, 1) and (2, 5)
2 (6, 16)

Aiming higher
1 There are **nine** isosceles triangles formed by joining:
a) (2, 2), (6, 4), (6, 0)
b) (2, 2), (6, 4), (10, 2)
c) (2, 2), (10, 2), (6, 0)
d) (6, 0), (6, 4), (10, 2)
e) (4, 9), (8, 9), (6, 4)
f) (4, 9), (8, 9), (6, 2)
g) (4, 9), (8, 9), (6, 0)
2 Any point with a y-co-ordinate of 3, e.g (3, 3) or (7, 3)

Using and applying
1 (0, 5) and (3, 9). E.g. To move from A to B is 3 squares along to the right and 4 squares up. So from B to the third point is 3 squares to the left and 4 squares up and the fourth point is opposite B
2 a) quadrilateral
b) For a parallelogram, e.g. move C to (6, 5)
c) For a trapezium, e.g. move C to (4, 5) or D to (2, 3)

Unit 14 Drawing shapes
On track
1 Check drawing
2 Check drawing

Aiming higher
1 A, B
2 a), b), c) Check drawings

Using and applying
1 A, B, D
2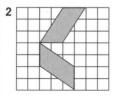

Unit 15 Moving shapes
On track
1 Flag B is facing the wrong way: False
The arrow on flag B is facing the wrong way: True
Flag B is too close to the mirror line: True

2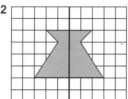

3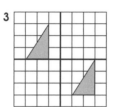

Aiming higher
1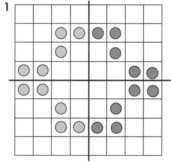

2

3

Using and applying
1 a) A to B: reflection in x-axis
b) A to D: reflection in y-axis
c) A to C: rotation about the origin of 180°; reflection in the y-axis followed by reflection in the x-axis; reflection in the x-axis followed by reflection in the y-axis

2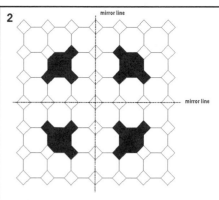

Unit 16 Angles
On track
1 a) 60°
b) Check drawing
c) 3rd angle = 70°
2 a) 40°
b) 110°

Aiming higher
1 24
2 A = 110°; B = 65°; C = 250°

Using and applying
1 210° or 150°
Explanation, e.g. 12 hours is 360° so 1 hour is 30° so 7 hours is 210°
2 Between 15° and 25°

Unit 17 Measurement
On track
1 a) 2.5 mm, 15 cm, 12 m, 1.5 km
b) 100 ml, 0.75 litres, 1500 ml, 1.6 litres 2 litres
c) $\frac{3}{4}$ kg, 1500 g, 1.6 kg, 2 kg, 10,000 g
2 1060 cm

Aiming higher
1 a) 200 cm, 350 cm, 2 cm
b) 20 mm, 55 mm, 2000 mm
c) 2000 g, 6350 g, 525 g
2 3.627 kg

Using and applying
1 a) 1050 m or 1.05 km
b) 2050 m or 2.05 km
2 e.g. There are 30 lots of 8 km in 240 km, so 30 times 5 = 150 miles

Unit 18 Reading and interpreting scales
On track
1 Check drawing

Aiming higher
1 700 ml or 0.7 litres
2 Total weight = 3.75 kg or 3750 g; 1 ball weighs 750 g

Using and applying
1 Jug weight is 125 g; jug + flour weight is 550 g, so by subtraction the flour weight is 425 g
2 Volume of jug is 1.2 litres or 1200 ml, so the number of glasses is 1200 ÷ 150 = 8

Unit 19 Area and perimeter
On track
1 a) Perimeter of flag = 3.6 m
b) Area of flag = 7200 cm²
c) Area of shaded triangle = 0.2 x 7200 = 1440 cm²

Aiming higher

1 Divide the shape into 2 rectangles, e.g.
8 x 2 and 6 x 2 = 16 + 12 = 28 cm², or think of the shape as a large square with a small square cut away:
area of large square = 8 x 8 = 64 cm², area of cut-away square = 6 x 6 = 36 cm², so area remaining, the L-shape, = 64 – 36 = 28 cm²

2 a) Side of large square = 15 + 5 = 20 cm
   Area of large square = 20 x 20 = 400 cm². There are 4 small triangles, each has an area of $\frac{1}{2}$ x 5 x 15 cm² so total blue area = 4 x $\frac{1}{2}$ x 5 x 15 = 150 cm².
  b) The shaded square has an area of 400 – 150 = 250 cm².

Using and applying

1 There are two ways of calculating the answer:
  (i) See how many tiles fit along the length and the width:
   65 ÷ 6.5 = 10, 36 ÷ 4.5 = 8, and 10 x 8 = 80 so 80 tiles
  (ii) Area of table top = 65 x 36 = 2340 cm²
   Area of tile = 6.5 x 4.5 = 29.25 cm²
   2340 ÷ 29.25 = 80 so 80 tiles

2 Perimeter = 32 cm. One side = 5 cm, so opposite sides added together = 10 cm. Therefore the other two sides added together = 22 cm, so one side = 11 cm. Therefore area = 5 x 11 = 55 cm².

Unit 20 Probability
On track

1 Check answers:
  a) could be anywhere
  b) A
  c) B
  d) C
  e) E

Aiming higher

1 a) NT
  b) T
  c) T
  d) T

Using and applying

1 a) ✓ Amy – 9 out of 20 are blue; Emily – 3 out of 10 are blue
  b) ✓ Emily – 6 out of 10 are red; Amy – 10 out of 20 are red

Unit 21 Interpreting data
On track

1 a) July; 22°C
  b) e.g. January and December; March and November
  c) e.g. Hottest month in Amsterdam is July, same as London, but temperature is 25°C so higher than in London; January is colder than December in Amsterdam; January in Amsterdam is the same temperature as London

Aiming higher

1 e.g. How many ate eggs? (7) Do more eat toast than cereal?

2 a) 31–40
  b) 5 + 7 + 20 + 25 +15 = 72
  c) 10 + 25 + 15 = 50

Using and applying

1 a) Cat is most popular and horse is least popular (largest and smallest sectors).
  b) Could also use a bar chart.

Unit 22 Frequency tables
On track

1 a)

Shoe size	Frequency
6	10
7	8
8	3

  b) Check bar chart

Aiming higher

1 a) 16
  b) red

Using and applying

1 a) $\frac{1}{4}$, 100
  b) No; the number of people is different – 400 in Derby and 800 in Nottingham
  c) 16 – 39

Unit 23 Averages
On track

1 13.9 seconds
2 The three numbers must total 36 so, e.g. 6, 10, 20 or 10, 12, 14.

Aiming higher

1 a) All four of the '5' cards must be left and the remaining three cards left could be all '3' cards or all '4'cards or a mixture of both.
  b) The mode of the cards removed will either be 3 or 4.

2 The mean of A and B is 50, so A + B = 100. A + B + C = 150, so 100 + C = 150 and C = 50.
   Hence A = 40 and B = 60 or 55 and 45 etc ... in fact, any two numbers that add to 100 (except 50 and 50).

Using and applying

1 a) 90
  b) 15
  c) Ruth is correct because Joan's mean score was less and the range of marks is greater, so Ruth is more consistent. Or Ruth's total for the five tests was 450, Joan's total was 445 so Ruth is better.

Unit 24 Patterns and sequences
On track

1 a) 999 x **15** = 14,985; 999 x **16** = **15,984**
  b) 12,987 ÷ 999 = 13
  c) Multiplying by 10 means the number must end in zero.

2 11, 15, 14, 18
   The numbers in the circles are in the 3 times table.

Aiming higher

1 a) 38 cm
  b) L = 2W + 2

2 a) 4, 5, 6 and 15 in the middle triangle
  b) Each number in the triangles goes up by 1. The centre number goes up by 3.
   N = A + B + C

Using and applying

1 a) 2.4 cm, 2.7 cm; the lengths increase by 0.3 cm each time
  b) 5.2 cm, 5.8 cm, 6.4 cm, 7 cm, 7.6 cm predict 8.2 cm – goes up in 0.6 cm steps
   Check = 1.1 + 1.1 + 3.0 + 3.0 = 8.2 cm

2 a) 6 spots along the top row and along the bottom row, 4 spots on the diagonal
  b) 7 spots along the top and bottom 5 spots on the diagonal making a total of 19
  c) Check drawing
  d) Number of spots along the top and bottom are 1 more than the shape number, spots in diagonal are 1 less than shape number

Design: Clive Sutherland

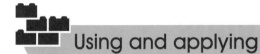 **Using and applying**

1 This is how Beth works out 15% of 360.

10% of 360 is 36.

5% of 360 is 18.

So 15% of 360 is 3 × 18 = 54.

Use Beth's method to work out 17.5% of 720.

2 Find two words in which 20% of the letters are vowels.

3 Max buys a flute that costs £400.

a) First he pays a deposit of 30%. How much is this?

b) Then he makes 12 monthly payments of £30. How much do these payments come to?

c) What is the total of the deposit and the monthly payments?

d) How much extra does he pay for the flute?

 4 Show how you can work out 65% of £80 without using a calculator.

5 The number of people going to the cinema increased from 72,000 in 1992 to 108,000 in 2002. Calculate the percentage increase in the number of people going to the cinema from 1992 to 2002.

12 2-D shapes and 3-D solids

What will you learn?

How to use the properties of parallel and perpendicular edges and faces to describe and classify 2-D shapes and 3-D solids

I know how to:

● identify, visualise and describe simple properties of rectangles, triangles, regular polygons and 3-D solids

● recognise parallel and perpendicular lines in grids and shapes.

I need to be able to:

● identify perpendicular or parallel edges or faces in 3-D solids.

Example

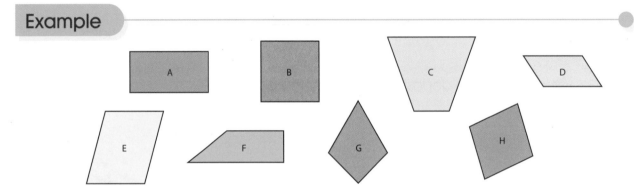

Which of these quadrilaterals is a:

square?	rectangle?	kite?	parallelogram?	trapezium?	rhombus?
B	*A*	*G*	*D, E, H*	*C, F*	*H*

Which of the quadrilaterals have two pairs of parallel lines?

● *A, B, D, E, H have two pairs of parallel lines.*

Key facts

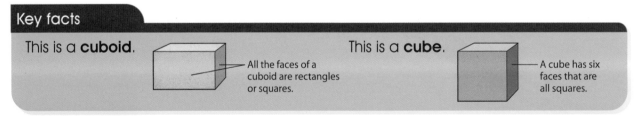

This is a **cuboid**.　　All the faces of a cuboid are rectangles or squares.

This is a **cube**.　　A cube has six faces that are all squares.

Language

Face　a flat side of a 3-D shape

Vertex (plural **vertices**)　a corner on a 3-D shape

Edge　the boundary between two faces on a 3-D shape

Side　the line joining two vertices on a 2-D shape

Quadrilateral　any 2-D shape with four straight sides

Parallel lines　remain the same distance apart along all of their length

Perpendicular lines　are at right angles to each other

On track

1 How many faces, edges and vertices does a cuboid have?

2 This picture shows a set of steps.

a) What solid shapes could they be made from?

b) How many vertical edges are there?

c) How many horizontal edges are there?

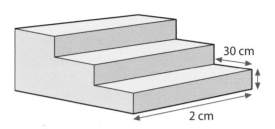
30 cm
2 cm

3 Each set of properties describes a type of triangle.

Copy and complete the table with the correct name for each triangle.

Properties	Triangle
● has one right angle ● can be isosceles	
● all three sides the same length ● all three angles the same size (equal to 60°)	
● two sides equal in length ● angles opposite the equal sides are equal	
● no sides are the same length ● no angles are equal	

4

    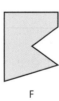

A   B   C   D   E   F

List the shapes that have:

a) two sets of two parallel lines   **b)** two sets of three parallel lines.

c) three sets of two parallel lines

Aiming higher

1 List as many of the properties of each quadrilateral as you can.

a) square   **b)** rectangle   **c)** parallelogram   **d)** rhombus   **e)** kite   **f)** trapezium

2 Name and describe shapes A to E as fully as you can.

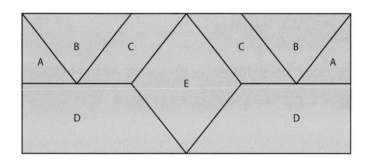

3 Look at the diagram opposite.

a) Which four triangles in the diagram together make a kite?

b) Write down a pair of triangles that will make a parallelogram.

Can you find a different pair?

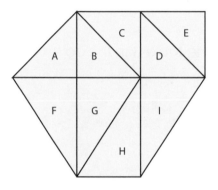

Using and applying

1 The quadrilateral has vertices A, B, C and D.

A is the point (2, 4), B is (6, 4), C is (10, 6) and D is (5, 7).

By moving one point, can you change the shape into:

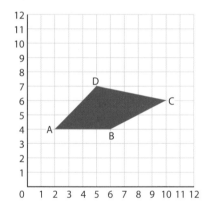

a) a parallelogram?

b) a triangle?

Write down the name of the point you are moving and the position it moves to.

2 A square-based pyramid has five faces and five vertices.

a) How many faces and vertices does a pyramid with a three-sided (triangular) base have? Do you know another name for pyramids with a triangular base?

b) How many faces and vertices does a pyramid with a five-sided base have?

c) Can you find a connection between the number of faces and vertices in a pyramid and the number of sides of its base?

13 Co-ordinates and shapes

What will you learn?

How to find the co-ordinates of an incomplete shape

I know how to:

● read and plot co-ordinates when the *x*-co-ordinate and the *y*-co-ordinate are both positive.

I need to be able to:

● work out co-ordinates of the end-points or mid-point of a line.

Example

Plot the points A (1, 4), B (2, 1) and C (4, 3) and join them to make an isosceles triangle. Write down the co-ordinates of the mid-point of the line BC.

Find the co-ordinates of a fourth point, D, so that ABCD is a parallelogram.

● *The mid-point of BC is (3, 2).*

● *D is the point (3, 6).*

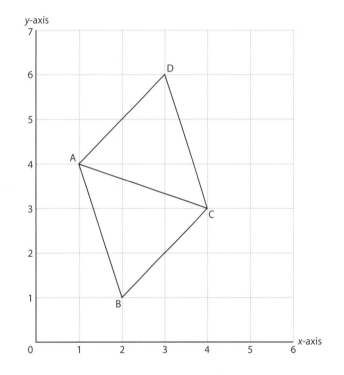

Key facts

The *x*-axis goes across the grid, the *y*-axis goes up.
Co-ordinates are written as a pair of numbers with the x-value coming first.
E.g. a point with co-ordinates (5, 4) is 5 units across and 4 units up from (0, 0).

Language

Axis (plural **axes**)   the line or lines on the grid that show the scale

Vertex (plural **vertices**) **on a 3-D shape**   a corner

Isosceles triangle   a triangle with two equal sides

On track

1 Look at the grid.

A and C are two vertices of a square.
X is the centre of the square.

Write down the co-ordinates of the
other corners of the square.

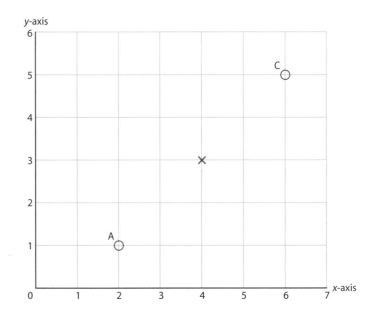

2 The shaded shape is an isosceles triangle.

What are the co-ordinates of the third vertex of the triangle?

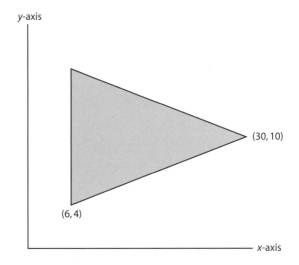

Aiming higher

1 Draw a co-ordinate grid on squared paper.

Plot these points.

(2, 2)   (6, 2)   (10, 2)   (6, 0)   (6, 4)   (4, 9)   (8, 9)

Join them up in threes to make as many isosceles triangles as you can.

How many triangles have you found?

2 A, B and C are the vertices of an isosceles triangle.

Write down the co-ordinates of another point P that would make A, B and P the vertices of an isosceles triangle.

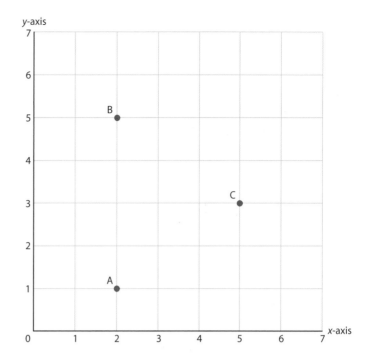

 Using and applying

1 Draw a co-ordinate grid on squared paper.

Plot the points A (3, 1) and B (6, 5) and join them with a straight line. The line makes one side of a rhombus.

Write down the co-ordinates of the other two vertices of the rhombus. Explain how you knew where these other vertices would be.

2 **a)** Draw a co-ordinate grid on squared paper.

Plot the points A (0, 0), B (4, 0), C (4, 3), D (2, 5).

Join A to B, B to C, C to D and D to A.

What shape have you made?

b) By moving one corner of the shape, you can change the shape into a parallelogram.

Move one corner and write down the new co-ordinates.

c) By moving one corner of the original shape, you can change it into a trapezium.

Write down which point you move and its new co-ordinates.

14 Drawing shapes

What will you learn?

How to make and draw shapes accurately

I am able to:

- draw nets of 3-D shapes
- use a set square and ruler to draw shapes with parallel and perpendicular sides
- use a protractor to draw an acute or an obtuse angle.

I need to learn how to:

- draw angles in shapes accurately
- use what I know about their properties when I draw shapes.

Example

Draw a straight line from point A to divide the shaded shape into a parallelogram and a right-angled triangle.

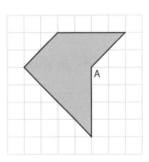

Now draw one more line to divide the shape into two trapeziums and two right-angled triangles.

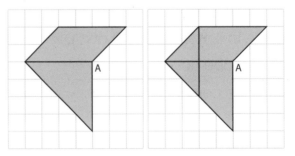

Key fact

The 2-D net of a 3-D shape will fold up to make the 3-D shape.

Language

Parallel lines remain the same distance apart along all of their length

Perpendicular lines are at right angles to each other

You need to know the names and properties of the common 2-D and 3-D shapes.

On track

1 Use your ruler and set square to draw a 6 cm by 8 cm rectangle.

2 Copy the diagram onto dotty or squared paper.

Add two more squares to complete a net for a cube.

Aiming higher

1 Which of these drawings are nets for a tetrahedron?

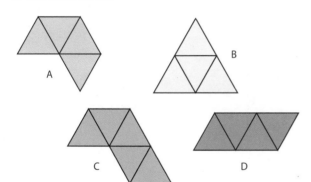

2 You need squared paper and a ruler.

a) Draw a triangle with one right angle.

b) Draw a quadrilateral with only two right angles.

c) Draw a pentagon with only three right angles.

Using and applying

1 Which of these drawings are nets for a square-based pyramid?

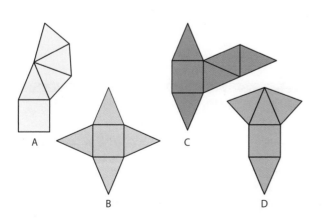

2 Copy the diagram onto squared paper.

Divide the L-shape into four smaller identical L-shapes.

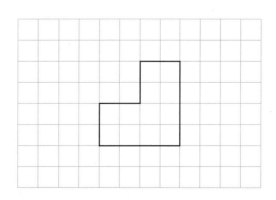

15 Moving shapes

What will you learn?

How to reflect, rotate and translate shapes on grids

I know how to:

- complete patterns with up to two lines of symmetry
- draw the position of a shape after a reflection or translation.

I need to be able to:

- visualise and draw where a shape will be after rotation through 90° or 180° about its centre or one of its vertices.

Example

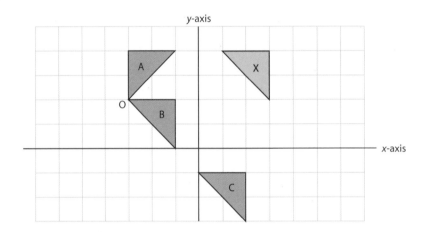

Triangles A, B and C show the position of triangle X after a translation or a reflection.

Describe the transformations.

- *Triangle C is a translation of triangle X, 1 square to the left and 5 squares down.*
- *Triangle A is a reflection of triangle X in the y-axis.*
- *Triangle B is a translation of triangle X, 4 squares to the left and 2 squares down.*
- *Triangle B is a rotation of 90° clockwise about the point O of triangle A.*

Key facts

A translation is described by the distance moved to the left or right, and the distance moved up or down.
A reflected shape is the same distance from, but on the opposite side of, the mirror line as the original shape and has been 'flipped over'.
A rotation should be written down with the angle turned through and the point about which the turn takes place.

Language

Translation   a move to left or right and/or up and down, with no turning or 'flipping'

Reflection   a 'flip over' movement in a mirror line

Rotation   a clockwise or anti-clockwise turn about a point

Transformation   the movement of a shape by translation, reflection or rotation

Symmetry   a shape has (line) symmetry if a mirror line can be placed so that the shape on one side reflects exactly onto the other side

 On track

1 Harry has drawn the reflection of flag A in the mirror line.

He labels its reflection B. His teacher marks it wrong.

Copy these possible reasons for it being wrong.

● Flag B is facing the wrong way.

● The arrow on flag B is facing the wrong way.

● Flag B is too close to the mirror line.

Think about each one and write *true* or *false* next to it.

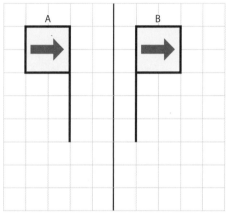

2 Copy the shape and the mirror line onto squared paper.

Draw the reflection of the shape in the mirror line.

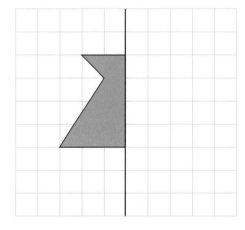

3 Draw the position of this triangle after it has been translated 4 squares to the right and 3 squares down.

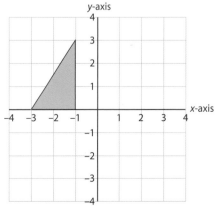

Aiming higher

1 Shagufta is making a pattern using pegs and a peg board.

She wants the pattern to have symmetry.

The left side is already complete and has one line of symmetry.

Copy the pattern so far onto squared paper. Draw in the line of symmetry.

Complete the pattern to make it symmetrical. Draw in the new line of symmetry.

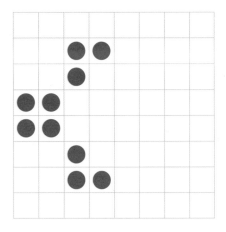

2 Copy the shape onto squared paper. Rotate it 90° clockwise about point X.

Draw the shape in its new position on the grid.

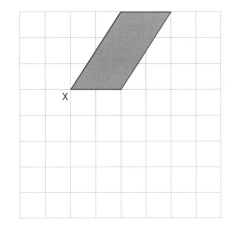

3 Copy this diagram onto squared paper and reflect the shape in the mirror line.

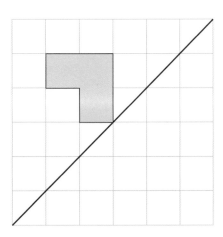

Using and applying

1 All of the L-shapes are identical.

Write down a transformation that moves the first shape onto the second shape:

a) A to B   **b)** A to D   **c)** A to C

There are three different transformations that will move A onto C. Can you find them all?

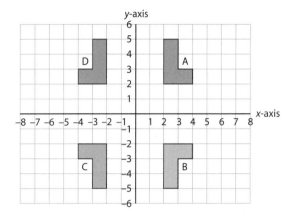

2 Complete the diagram below to make a shape that is symmetrical about both mirror lines.

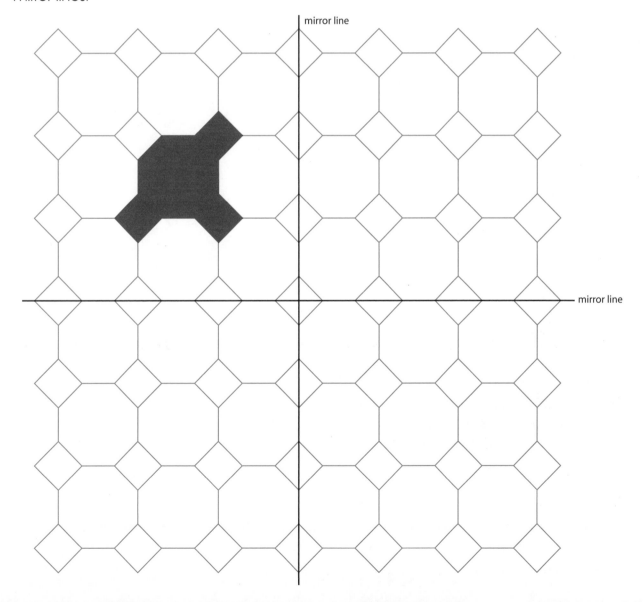

16 Angles

What will you learn?

That the angle sum of a triangle is 180° and the sum of angles around a point is 360°

I know how to:

- estimate angles
- use a protractor to measure and draw them
- calculate the angles on a straight line.

I need to be able to:

- calculate the angles in a triangle or around a point.

Example

Two of the angles in a triangle are 35° and 45°.

What is the size of the third angle?

- *Angles in a triangle add up to 180°.*

    35° + 45° = 80°

    So the third angle = 180° − 80° = 100°

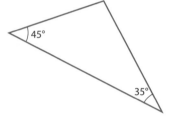

There are nine equal angles around a point.

What is the size of each angle?

- *Angles around a point add up to 360°.*

    The nine angles are equal.

    So each angle is 360° ÷ 9 = 40°.

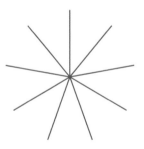

Key facts

Angles in a triangle add up to 180°.
Angles on a straight line add up to 180°.
Angles around a point add up to 360°.
Angles in an equilateral triangle each measure 60°.
Two angles in an isosceles triangle are equal: these are the angles opposite the equal sides.

Language

Perpendicular lines are at right angles to each other
Vertical lines are **perpendicular** to **horizontal** lines

On track

1 **a)** Estimate the size of this angle and then measure it to the nearest degree.

b) Draw a line at an angle of 50° to A to make a triangle.

c) What size should the third angle of the triangle be?

d) Measure it on your drawing. How accurate were you?

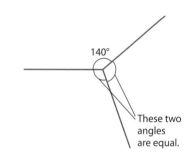

2 **a)** Calculate the size of the third angle in the triangle.

b) Find the missing angles around the point.

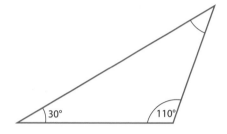

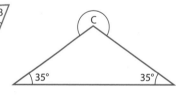

These two angles are equal.

Aiming higher

1 There are a number of equal angles around a point.

The size of each angle is 15°. How many equal angles are there?

2 Find the values of angles A, B and C.

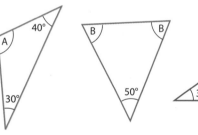

Using and applying

1 What is the angle between the hands of a clock at seven o'clock?

Explain how you know.

2 For safety the angle between this ladder and the ground must be between 65° and 75°.

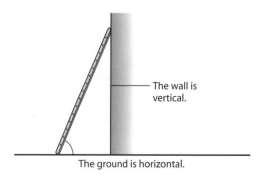

The wall is vertical.

The ground is horizontal.

Between what values must the angle between the ladder and the wall be?

17 Measurement

What will you learn?

How to convert from one unit of measure to another using decimals

I know how to:

- convert larger to smaller units using decimals to one place.

I need to be able to:

- convert between units using decimals to two places.

Example

Put these weights in order, smallest first.

1.2 kg   1500 g   160 g   2000 g   0.8 kg

- *First change weights into grams:*

  1.2 kg = 1.2 × 1000 = 1200 g, 0.8 kg = 0.8 × 1000 = 800 g.

  The order is 160 g, 800 g,   1200 g,   1500 g,   2000 g.

- *Now write the weights using the original units:*

  160 g,   0.8 kg,   1.2 kg,   1500 g,   2000 g.

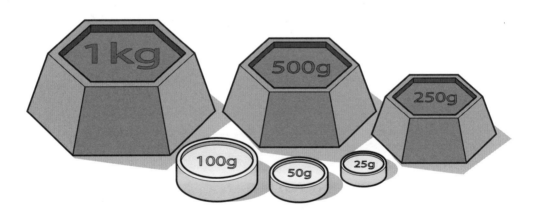

Key facts

10 mm in 1 cm	100 cm in 1 m	1000 m in 1 km
1000 g in 1 kg	1000 ml in 1 litre	

Language

centi ...   in measurement means a hundredth

kilo ...   in measurement means a thousand

On track

1 **a)** Write these lengths in order, shortest first:

15 cm   12 m   1.5 km   2.5 mm

b) Put these volumes in order, smallest first.

2 litres   1500 ml   1.6 litres   100 ml   0.75 litres

c) Put these weights in order, smallest first.

2 kg   1500 g   1.6 kg   10,000 g $\frac{3}{4}$ kg

2 A tiger is 240 cm long.

A cheetah is 1.3 m long.

What is the difference in length between the tiger
and the cheetah, measured in cm?

Aiming higher

1 **a)** Change these lengths to
centimetres.

2 m   3.5 m   20 mm

b) Change these lengths to millimetres.

2 cm   5.5 cm   2 m

c) Change these weights to grams.

2 kg   6.35 kg   0.525 kg

2 Harry buys:
- a bag of potatoes weighing 1.5 kg
- a bunch of bananas weighing 900 g
- a bag of sugar weighing 1 kg and a
  packet of coffee weighing 227 g.

What is the weight of his shopping, in
kilograms?

Using and applying

1 Here is a signpost in a country park.

a) How much further is it to the cave than the
car park?

b) Helen is at the cave. How far would she have to
walk to the picnic site?

2 The distance from Ayton to Exton is **240 km**.

5 miles is approximately **8 km**.

Use this fact to calculate the approximate distance
in **miles** from Ayton to Exton.

Show how you worked it out.

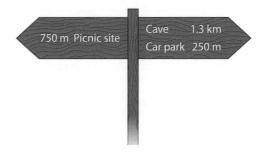

18 Reading and interpreting scales

What will you learn?

How to read scales and give my answers as accurately as the question asks

I know how to:

- work out a reading on a scale between two un-numbered divisions.

I need to be able to:

- compare readings on different scales.

Example

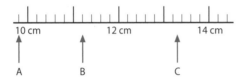

The diagram shows part of the scale on a metre rule.

Write down the values that arrows A, B and C are pointing to, correct to one place of decimals.

- *You need to look at the different size markings on the scale. There are slightly longer markings shown at 10 cm, 12 cm and 14 cm, and also at 11 cm and 13 cm although these are not labelled.*

- *There are four smaller markings between each centimetre marking, so there are five small steps from 10 cm to 11 cm, from 11 cm to 12 cm and so on. Each small step is 0.2 cm.*

- *A is pointing at 9.8 cm, B at 11.2 cm and C at 13.3 cm.*

Key facts

The measurements on scales can be very different.
Remember that there are 1000 g in a kilogram, 1000 ml in a litre.
Count the number of divisions to decide on the values of the marks that are labelled.

Language

There is no new vocabulary. You will be using and reading words like weight, volume, scale …

On track

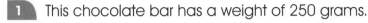

1 This chocolate bar has a weight of 250 grams.

On centimetre squared paper, draw a straight line scale from 0 to 1.5 kg.

Use 1 cm for every 100 g.

Make a mark at every 100 g, a shorter mark at every 50 g and a longer mark at every 500 g.

Label the 500 g marks. Don't forget 0.

Draw an arrow ↓ on the scale to show the reading for 250 g.

Temptation

Aiming higher

1 This is the scale on the side of a measuring jar.

There is some coloured water in the jar.

How much more water is needed to make 2 litres?

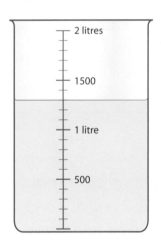

2 The picture shows five balls in a weighing pan.

What is the reading on the scale?

Each ball has the same weight.

What does each ball weigh? Write your answer in grams.

Using and applying

1 This scale shows the weight of a jug.

The scale below shows the weight of the same jug after some flour has been added.

How much flour has been added to the jug?

How did you work it out?

2 How many glasses each holding 150 ml can be filled from this jug of orange juice?

How did you work it out?

19 Area and perimeter

What will you learn?

How to estimate or calculate the perimeter and area of any shape

I know how to:

- use the formula for finding the area of a rectangle
- measure and calculate the perimeter of regular and irregular polygons.

I need to be able to:

- calculate the area and perimeter of shapes made from rectangles
- estimate the area of an irregular shape by counting squares.

Example

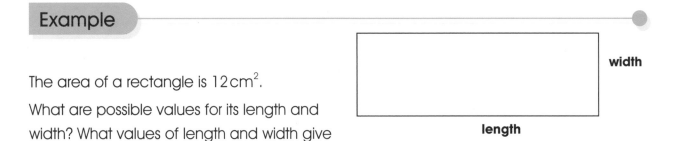

The area of a rectangle is $12\,cm^2$.

What are possible values for its length and width? What values of length and width give the smallest perimeter?

- *Area of a rectangle = length × width. Write down all the pairs of whole numbers that multiply to give 12 (the factor pairs): 1 and 12; 2 and 6; 3 and 4.*

- *Think of fraction and decimal pairs, e.g. $\frac{1}{2}$ and 24, $1\frac{1}{2}$ and 8; 2.4 and 5.*

- *One number in each pair could be the length, the other the width.*

- *Work out perimeters for each pair of numbers (2 × length + 2 × width):*

  $\frac{1}{2}$ and 24 gives 49 cm; 1 and 12 gives 26 cm; 2 and 6 gives 16 cm; 2.4 and 5 gives 14.8 cm; 3 and 4 gives 14 cm; $1\frac{1}{2}$ and 8 gives 19 cm.

- *From the list, the smallest perimeter occurs when length = 4 cm and width = 3 cm.*

Key facts

Area is measured in square units, e.g. square centimetres (cm^2).
Perimeter is a length so is measured in centimetres or metres or …

Language

Perimeter   is the distance around the edge of a flat shape
Area   is the amount of surface covered by the flat shape

 **On track**

1 This is a picture of a flag.

a) Work out its perimeter in metres.

b) Work out its area in cm².

c) 20% of the area of the flag is a triangle shaded grey.

What is the area of the shaded triangle?

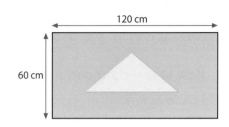

120 cm

60 cm

Aiming higher

1 Find the area and perimeter of this L-shape.
Show how you calculated your answers.

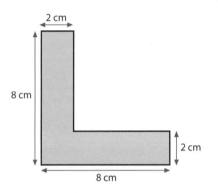

2 cm

8 cm

2 cm

8 cm

2 The diagram shows a shaded square inside a large square.

a) Calculate the area of the large square.

b) Calculate the area of the smaller shaded square.

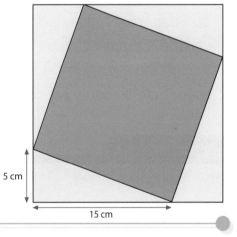

5 cm

15 cm

 Using and applying

1 Here are some tiles. Each tile measures 4.5 cm by 6.5 cm.

6.5 cm

4.5 cm

Michelle uses the tiles to cover the top of
a rectangular table measuring 65 cm by 36 cm.

How many tiles does she need? Show how you worked it out.

2 A rectangle has a perimeter of 32 cm. One side measures 5 cm.

Calculate the area of the rectangle. Show your working.

20 Probability

What will you learn?

How to use data and the language of chance to solve problems

I know how to:

- describe what chance there is of something happening.

I need to be able to:

- look at data and predict what might happen using words about likelihood, e.g. certain, impossible.

Example

Look at the spinners. If you need to score 4 to win a game, which spinner would you choose?

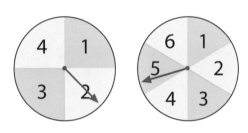

- *The answer would be the left-hand spinner since '4' covers $\frac{1}{4}$ of the circle while on the other spinner '4' covers only $\frac{1}{6}$ of the circle.*

- *Remember to look carefully at how drawings are labelled and divided. If the question was 'If you need to score an even number to win, which spinner would you choose?', there is actually no difference. Although the left-hand spinner looks as though the even numbers might cover more area and give a better chance, they cover half the circle just as on the right-hand spinner.*

Key fact

The chance of something happening is measured by reference to a scale.

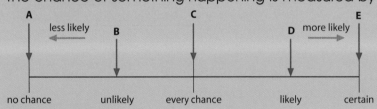

Language

Impossible   no chance, cannot happen (A on the probability scale)

Certain   sure to happen (E on the probability scale)

Even chance   (or evens) just as likely as unlikely (C on the probability scale)

Likely   more than an even chance but not certain (D on the probability scale)

Unlikely   less than an even chance but not impossible (B on the probability scale)

On track

1 Here is a probability scale.

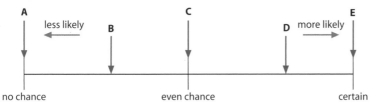

Match each of these events to an arrow on the line (A, B, C, D, E or F):

a) You will watch TV tonight.

b) You will be 21 years old next year.

c) The next person to come into the classroom with be left-handed.

d) When you throw a 2p coin it will land on heads.

e) When you throw a 2p coin it will land on heads or tails.

Aiming higher

1 Here are three spinners.

Which of these statements is **true** (T)?

Which of these statements is **not true** (NT)?

a) You are more likely to get a 2 on spinner A than spinner B.

b) You are more likely to get a 3 on spinner B than on the other two spinners.

c) You are just as likely to get a 1 on spinner A as on spinner C.

d) You are unlikely to get a 1 on spinner B.

Using and applying

1 Emily has a bag with 10 counters in it: 6 are red, 3 are blue and 1 is green.

Amy has a bag with 20 counters in it: 10 are red, 9 are blue and 1 is green.

Emily and Amy each choose a counter from their own bag without looking.

Copy each statement and put a tick ✓ if it is true. Put a cross ✗ if it is not true.

a) Amy is more likely than Emily to choose a blue counter.

b) Emily is more likely than Amy to choose a red counter.

Explain each decision. Don't forget to think about the total numbers of counters in each bag.

21 Interpreting data

What will you learn?

How to solve problems by collecting and interpreting data, drawing conclusions and identifying further questions to ask

I know how to:

● collect and present data in different ways.

I need to be able to:

● use my results to solve problems

● use ICT to present my data.

Example

Amy asked some people about their favourite fruits.

This bar chart shows how they answered.

Suggest two questions that you could ask about this data and give the answers to your questions.

● *How many people chose pears?* [13]

● *Which fruit was chosen by the fewest people?* (apple)

● *How many people did Amy ask?* [52]

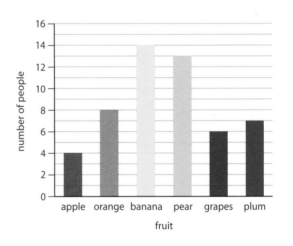

Key facts

You must have equal intervals along each scale.
It does not always make sense to join up points in a line graph. Think carefully before you do it.

Language

Tally chart   a table that counts 'how many' by using tally marks, e.g. 𝍩 counts 5

Bar chart   see **Example** question

Pie chart   see question 1 in **Aiming higher**

Line graph   see question 1 in **On track**

On track

1 This graph shows the average monthly temperature in London.

a) What was the hottest month and what was the average temperature in that month?

b) Name two months in which the average temperature was the same.

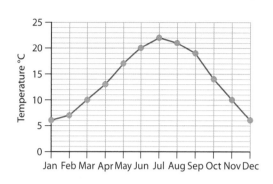

This graph shows the average monthly temperature in Amsterdam.

c) Write down two results that allow you to compare the temperatures in both cities.

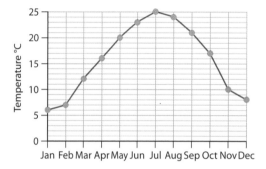

Aiming higher

1 This pie chart shows the favourite breakfast food of 28 pupils.

Suggest two questions you could ask about the data in this graph.

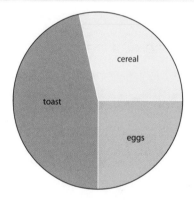

2 This graph shows the marks scored in a test by children in Class 5 and in Class 6.

a) What was the most common score in the test?

b) How many children took the test?

c) Estimate how many got more than half marks.

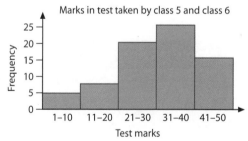

Using and applying

1 This pie chart shows how popular some pets are in Nottingham.

a) What were the most popular and least popular pets? How do you know?

b) How else could you show the data?

22 Frequency tables

What will you learn?

How to construct and interpret frequency tables, bar charts with grouped discrete data, line graphs and how to interpret pie charts

I know how to:

● construct frequency tables, pictograms and bar and line graphs.

I need to be able to:

● construct and interpret bar charts with grouped data

● interpret pie charts.

Example

Mrs Khan asked the 27 pupils in her class, 'How many children are in your family?'

Here are their answers:

2	2	2	1	1	3	2	2	1	1	3	4	2	1
1	2	2	1	3	3	2	2	1	1	2	1	2	

Mrs Khan recorded the answers in a tally chart.

Complete the tally chart and draw a bar chart to show the results.

Number of children	Tally	Total
1	ЖЖ ЖЖ	10
2	ЖЖ ЖЖ //	12
3	////	4
4	/	1

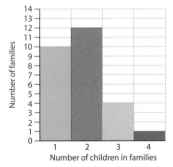

Key facts

You must have equal intervals along each scale.
It does not always make sense to join up points in a line graph. Think carefully before you do it.

Language

Tally chart   see **Example** question

Bar chart   see **Example** question

Pie chart   see question 1 in **Using and applying**

Grouped data   the data or numbers are collected together into groups, see question 1 in **Using and applying**

Discrete data   data that can be found by counting; if data is from measurement, it is continuous data

On track

1 Sally asked each person in her class for the size of their shoes. Here are the results.

7	5	6	8	4	5
6	7	8	7	5	6
6	5	7	6	6	8
7	5	6	6	7	7
5	6	5	5	6	7

a) Copy and complete this frequency table.

Shoe size	Tally	Frequency
4	/	1
5	///// ///	8
6	///// /////	
7		
8		

b) Draw a bar chart to show the sizes.

Aiming higher

1 Sally did a survey to find a favourite rainbow colour for some children at her school.

She showed the results for the boys and girls separately.

a) How many pupils altogether chose yellow?

b) Which was the most popular colour for the boys?

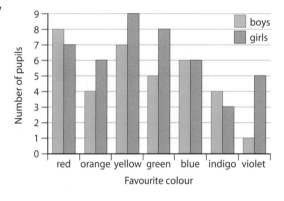

Using and applying

1 These two pie charts show information from a survey of people's ages.

In the survey 400 people from Derby and 800 people in Nottingham were asked their ages.

a) Roughly what fraction of people in Derby were under 16?

About how many people is this?

b) Amy says that the charts show that the same number of people were under 16 in both places. Is she right? How do you know?

c) What is the smallest age group in Nottingham?

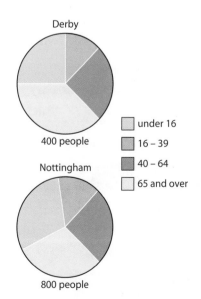

Derby
400 people

Nottingham
800 people

□ under 16
□ 16 – 39
■ 40 – 64
□ 65 and over

23 Averages

What will you learn?

How to calculate the mean of a set

I know that:

- the median and the mode are two types of average
- the median is the middle number and the mode is the most common number.

I need to be able to:

- add up numbers correctly and divide one number by another number to find the mean, another type of average
- put a list of numbers in order, smallest to largest, to find the median.

Example

The children in Year 6 had an English test. Mr Smith gave them their marks after he had put them in order:

100   95   90   85   80   75   75   70   65

- The shaded mark in the middle, 80, is the **median**.
- The mark which occurred most often, 75, is the **mode**.
- The **mean** mark is found by:

  adding together all the marks:

  100 + 95 + 90 + 85 + 80 + 75 + 75 + 70 + 65 = 735

  and then dividing by the number of marks:

  *735 ÷ 9 = 81.67, so the **mean** = 81.67.*

- The **range** is the smallest number subtracted from the largest number

  = 100 – 65 = 35.

Key fact

The mean of a set of data is found by adding the data and dividing the total by the number of data.

Language

Mean   is the numbers added together, divided by how many numbers there are

Mode   is the most common number in a list

Median   is the middle number in an ordered list

Range   is the smallest number subtracted from the largest number

On track

1 Linford runs 100 metres 12 times.

These are his times in seconds.

13.5   13.7   13.9   13.6

14.1   14.4   13.9   13.8

13.7   13.7   14.5   14.2

What is his mean (average) time?

2 Write three different numbers so that the mean of the three numbers is 12.

Aiming higher

1 a) Copy these numbers from the cards. Cross out five of them so that the mode of the numbers left is 5.

5   3   4   4   5   3   3   4   3   5   5   3

b) What is the mode of the numbers on the cards you crossed out?

2 A, B and C stand for three different numbers.

The mean of A and B is 50.   The mean of A and C is 45.   A + B + C = 150

Calculate the values of A, B and C.

Using and applying

1 Ruth's scores in mathematics tests last year were 83, 86, 98, 87 and 96.

a) Calculate Ruth's mean score.

b) Calculate the range of Ruth's scores.

Joan took the same tests. Her mean score was 89 and the range was 20.

c) Ruth says that she did better than Joan. Is Ruth correct?

24 Patterns and sequences

What will you learn?

How to describe and explain sequences, patterns and relationships

I know how to:

● explore patterns and relationships.

I need to be able to:

● construct and use simple expressions and formulae in words, then symbols.

Example

Here is a sequence of shapes made with matchsticks.

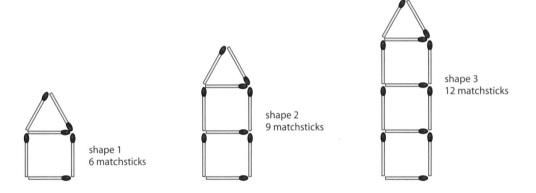

shape 1
6 matchsticks

shape 2
9 matchsticks

shape 3
12 matchsticks

The sequence continues in the same way.

Calculate how many matchsticks there will be in shape 10.

● *E.g. each shape has three more matchsticks than the previous shape, so count on in 3s from 12. This means that shape 4 has 15 matchsticks, shape 5 has 18, … shape 10 has 33.*

● *Or you may recognise that the number of matchsticks is the three times table + 3. This means that shape 10 has 10 × 3 + 3 = 33.*

Key fact

Always look for the difference between one number in the sequence and the next.

Language

Sequences are arrangements of numbers or shapes that change in the same way from one 'term' in the sequence to the next

On track

1 **a)** Look at the way the digits change in this number pattern.

Use the pattern to copy and complete the pattern.

$$999 \times 12 = 11,988$$
$$999 \times 13 = 12,987$$
$$999 \times 14 = 13,986$$
$$999 \times \text{....} = 14,985$$
$$999 \times \text{....} = \text{.........}$$

b) Use the pattern to write down the answer to $12,987 \div 999$

c) Amy has written down the answer to 999×20 as 19,982.

How do you know she is wrong without doing any calculations?

2 Continue this number pattern by writing down the next four numbers.

Write down something that you notice about the numbers in the circles.

Aiming higher

1 Here are some picture sizes.

width in cm	10	15	20	25
length in cm	22	32	42	52

width

length

a) What is the length of a picture which has a width of 18 cm?

b) For each picture the length (**L**) is **twice** the width (**W**) add 2. Write this in symbols.

2 **a)** Copy the last triangle and fill in the missing numbers to continue the pattern.

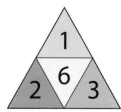 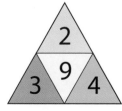 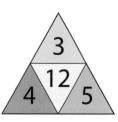 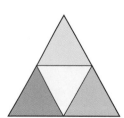

Explain how you worked out the missing numbers.

b) You could write letters in the spaces like this:

Then the rule is: Find out what N is by adding A, B and C together.

Write this rule just using the letters N, A, B and C.

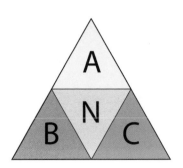

 Using and applying

1 Here is a set of rectangles. All of the rectangles have the same width.

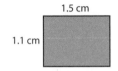 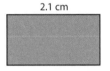  

1.5 cm   1.8 cm   2.1 cm

1.1 cm

a) What are the lengths of the next two rectangles. How do you know?

b) Find the perimeter of each of the five rectangles.

Predict what the perimeter will be for the sixth rectangle.

Now check your prediction. Show your calculations.

2 Look carefully to see how this pattern of spots is built up.

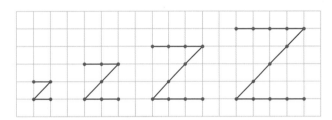

a) How would you make the next shape?

b) How many spots do you think are in the sixth shape?

c) Check your answer to **b)** by drawing the sixth shape.

d) What is the rule for making these patterns of dots?